HOW
LONG
IS
NOW?

Also by Tim Freke

THE GOSPEL OF THE SECOND COMING (with Peter Gandy)

LUCID LIVING

O O O

The titles above are available at your local bookstore,
or may be ordered by visiting:

Hay House USA: **www.hayhouse.com®**
Hay House Australia: **www.hayhouse.com.au**
Hay House UK: **www.hayhouse.co.uk**
Hay House South Africa: **www.hayhouse.co.za**
Hay House India: **www.hayhouse.co.in**

HOW
LONG
IS
NOW?

A Journey to Enlightenment
. . . and Beyond

TIM FREKE

HAY HOUSE, INC.
Carlsbad, California • New York City
London • Sydney • Johannesburg
Vancouver • Hong Kong • New Delhi

Published and distributed in the United States by: Hay House, Inc.: www.hayhouse .com • *Published and distributed in Australia by:* Hay House Australia Pty. Ltd.: www .hayhouse.com.au • *Published and distributed in the United Kingdom by:* Hay House UK, Ltd.: www.hayhouse.co.uk • *Published and distributed in the Republic of South Africa by:* Hay House SA (Pty), Ltd.: www.hayhouse.co.za • *Distributed in Canada by:* Raincoast: www.raincoast.com • *Published in India by:* Hay House Publishers India: www.hayhouse.co.in

Design: Tricia Breidenthal

Library of Congress Cataloging-in-Publication Data

Freke, Timothy.
  How long is now? : a journey to Enlightenment ... and beyond / Tim Freke. -- 1st ed.
    p. cm.
  ISBN 978-1-4019-2480-5 (tradepaper : alk. paper) 1. Spirituality. I. Title.
  BL624.F738 2009
  204'.4--dc22
                                    2009017177

ISBN: 978-1-4019-2480-5

12 11 10 09   4 3 2 1
1st edition, August 2009

Printed in the United States of America

Author's Note: Although I hail from the U.K., this book is being simultaneously published throughout the English-speaking world, which is why in this version, the spelling, grammar, and syntax are in colloquial American English.

CONTENTS

PROLOGUE

The Fabulous Story of One and All

My life has brought me to this moment. I am here and now. But where is here? Is it the spot beneath my feet . . . or the room I am sitting in . . . or the country I inhabit . . . or the whole universe? And how long is now? Is it this breath . . . or this particular day . . . or my lifetime . . . or forever?

I want to tell you about the extraordinary events of my life and what they have taught me about living in love with the ever-present, ever-changing moment. But where should I begin? "Tim" has been enjoying this magical mystery tour we call "life" for a little more than 49 years . . . some 2,500 weeks. But my story begins long before, because Tim's brief adventures can only be understood within the context of the grandiose story of life itself.

In this book, I want to take you on a philosophical journey of discovery into the mystery of the moment by sharing with you some personal experiences that have led me to profound ideas. But I think that it will be fun to start our time together by going back before time . . . to tell you a fabulous story about all that has led to us being here and now.

This story is an epic saga about the evolution of conscious-ness, the rise and fall of empires, and the inexplicable allure of game shows on daytime TV. It's a strange and poignant tale about you . . . and me . . . and *everything*. I'm going to give you a heavily abridged version, because to tell the whole thing would take forever

. . . literally. And it won't be an easy story to tell, since it's impossible to really put into words. But what the hell—let's go for it anyway.

The Evolution of Consciousness

Once upon a timeless now, there existed the mysterious source of all that is. The source was an infinite nothing, pregnant with the possibility for everything . . . the possibility of quarks and galaxies, inanimate matter and sentient life, unconscious nature and conscious reflection . . . the possibility of seeing and feeling, of fearing and hoping, of thinking and loving . . . the possibility of beautiful art and terrible cruelty, of justice and genocide, of lies and wisdom . . . the possibility for you and me . . . the possibility for this moment right now.

Before the beginning, there was a primal imagination with the power to imagine everything . . . so that's exactly what it did. Everything is a lot to imagine, so it started with some basics and worked its way up to more complex things. First up was the idea of "time," because it takes time to imagine everything. And with "time" came the idea of "space," because if you want stuff you've got to have somewhere to put it all.

There was also energy and light. And tiny particles that combined to form swirling constellations of stars. And self-organizing cells that cooperated to become flora and fauna. Like any innovative process, this was a continual dialectic between creating and criticizing, bold experimenting and ruthless editing, stupendous successes and disappointing dead ends.

The process of evolution may have been hit or miss, but it was definitely heading in a particular direction. The forms became more and more complex, and as they did, they also became more and more conscious. Eventually, the primal imagination conceived of sentient beings through whom the universe could look at itself, hear itself, touch itself, as well as—by necessity—eat itself.

It was only a matter of time before some big-brained bipeds called "human beings" became self-conscious. These clever monkeys were not only conscious of the world around them, they were also conscious that they were conscious. And they started to ask some pretty interesting questions, such as "Who am I?" "Why am I here?" and "Where did everything come from?" And this brings us to the dilemma that gives dramatic tension to our story. . . .

The Illusion of Separateness

Before the beginning, the primal imagination was like a big mind slumbering in the unconscious nothingness of deep sleep. Then it started to dream the adventure of life; as it did, it became conscious through each of the forms it was imagining itself to be. As a hippo, it experienced itself to be a hippo. As a hummingbird, it experienced itself to be a hummingbird. As a human being, it experienced itself to be a human being. And this is what created the illusion of separateness.

Human beings presumed that they were no more than the separate individuals they appeared to be in the life-dream. They had no idea that, in reality, all was one, because everything was an expression of the primal awareness that was dreaming up the universe. This cosmic case of mistaken identity would just be comical if it weren't for the fact that the illusion of separateness caused such huge amounts of suffering.

You see, when a brainy monkey believed: "I am a separate someone," this inevitably led to a preoccupation with its own self-interest. It wanted what was best for itself, its family, and its tribe. The result was division and conflict, oppressors and oppressed, slavery and empire. The dream of life was turning into a nightmare.

Religion, Science, and Consumerism

And there was something else that made matters worse. People came up with stories to make sense of life, since otherwise they wouldn't have had any idea about who they were and what to do next. Without much to go on, they created some remarkably stupid stories. And as their stories were the maps by which they navigated their lives, people's crazy beliefs led to some really crazy actions.

Men and women pictured an array of supernatural beings who were running the cosmos . . . gods of thunder and rain and fertility and, of course, war. They imagined that the gods of their tribe would help them plunder their neighbors. And so that's what they did.

At some point, the idea that there really was just one God started to become fashionable. On the face of it, you'd think this was a step in the right direction; but, alas, it was not. This God was imagined as a divine ruler of the cosmos who was depressingly similar to the vicious bullies who had set themselves up as kings and emperors here on Earth.

God was seen as a lawmaker with a large book of rules that he wanted his subjects to comply with, for which they would be rewarded with his favor. But he was a ruthless tyrant who would brutally torture all those who didn't worship and obey him. And he was all in favor of his pious devotees doing his dirty work for him. So they did . . . enthusiastically.

It took a heck of a long time, but eventually thinking people realized that religion was getting them nowhere. So they began to wonder if they should stop just making up stories arbitrarily according to taste and start paying attention to their actual experience of the world.

This was a period called "the Enlightenment," although in fact it was still pretty "endarkened." It saw some remarkable individuals strutting their stuff, waging a war of ideas against superstition and dogma. They did this by insisting that it was not enough to believe something just because everyone else believed it, or because you liked the idea, or because you were too lazy to come up with anything better. You needed a good reason to believe something. And the fact that you were told to believe something in an old book, or by some self-proclaimed prophet who was channeling messages from God, didn't qualify as a "good reason."

Once people began adopting this "empirical" approach, things started to speed up big-time. Some really smart scientists came up with a lot of astonishing ideas about the way the universe works, and people suddenly found that they could communicate over vast distances and fly through the air in gigantic metal tubes. And the sky wasn't the limit . . . because they even took a jaunt into outer space.

This all would have been great, but there was a problem. People were still lost in the illusion of separateness, and now they banded together in competing megatribes. So innovative technologies led to bigger, badder weapons that they could fight with on a global battlefield. The life-dream was getting much better and much worse at the same time.

On top of all of the problems in the outer world, there was a psychological crisis mushrooming in the dark recesses of the human soul. Science was very good at explaining *how* things were, but had nothing to say about *why* things were. So as the scientific worldview became trendy, life started looking increasingly meaningless and bleak. The universe it pictured was so incomprehensibly huge and inconceivably old that human beings felt insignificantly small.

Lots of people coped by adopting an "enjoy it while you can" approach to life. They distracted themselves by purchasing lots of shiny new things and reading glossy magazines about celebrity trivia. The purpose of life became to accumulate stuff, look good in jeans, and watch game shows. Thirteen billion years of evolution had finally led to *Who Wants to Be a Millionaire?*

But none of this compares to the problems that now started to loom large on the horizon. The consumerist boom had been fueled by energy created from ancient sunlight, which had been photosynthesized by primordial plants, which had become transformed into oceans of oil hidden within the earth. It was as if the primal imagination had laid down in advance the resources necessary to create the modern world. This allowed the evolutionary process to really heat up, but it also started heating up the environment, with potentially catastrophic consequences.

The underlying cause of all of these escalating problems was the illusion of separateness. People believed they were separate from each other, so they waged war. They believed they were separate from nature, so they laid waste their environment. They believed they were separate from the source of all, so they felt cast adrift in an alien world.

Waking Up to Oneness

Occasionally, however, throughout the game of *Chutes and Ladders* that is human history, certain individuals experienced something shocking that led them to see their predicament very differently. They found themselves entering an ultraconscious state that could be called being "deep awake." And this led them to a momentous realization:

> Life is like a dream and, although we appear to be separate individuals in the life-dream, in reality there is one awareness dreaming itself to be everyone and everything, and meeting itself in all its various forms.

Those who experienced this momentous realization found that it utterly transformed their experience of life because when they woke up to oneness, they found themselves unconditionally in love with life. And this led them to say some unintentionally provocative things, such as:

> "If you become more conscious, it will be like coming around from a coma. You'll remember that you're alive. You'll discover who you really are. You'll know that all is one. And you'll fall in love with the present moment."

Unfortunately, this didn't go down too well with the vast majority of humanity. If there's one thing unconscious people hate, it's being *told* that they're unconscious. So those who had awakened to oneness and love were condemned as troublemakers who should be quietly ignored or, better still, put to death.

Yet these largely unremembered men and women are the great heroes of our story. They were the trailblazers for a new stage of evolution that is beginning to really take off right now. Thus far in the human adventure, the possibility of waking up to oneness has not been taken seriously by mainstream culture, but in the 21st century, this is beginning to change.

This is occurring as a natural expression of the evolutionary imperative, just like all of the other transformations that have happened before it. As time goes by, more and more individuals are recognizing that things are not what they seem and are beginning to become deep awake. And I'm telling you this story because I have a hunch that you may be one of them.

Deep Asleep to Deep Awake

So our story starts with unconscious awareness in a state of deep sleep, and it climaxes with some ultraconscious individuals who are deep awake. The dream of separateness is the primal awareness progressing from unconscious oneness to conscious oneness.

A Journey to this Moment

And that's a brief synopsis of the plot so far. It's been an awesome journey to get us to this present moment. The universe spent an incredibly long time in a gaseous state. It also got sidetracked for millions of years into the dead end of dinosaurs. But it finally got to self-conscious beings capable of waking up to oneness.

The pioneers of awakening have cleared a narrow path to this ultraconscious state, which has allowed others to make the journey more easily. Now those who are following in their footsteps are in the process of transforming this narrow esoteric path, designed for a mystical elite, into an enormous freeway open to all, so we can collectively wake up to oneness and love the dream of life.

What's going to happen next? As things stand, the story is getting to the exciting part. Everything is in the balance. Are we so lost in the illusion of separateness that we will sleepwalk into disaster? Or will we wake up and find compassionate solutions to our problems? It's hard to say. But the cool thing is that you and I get to play a role in governing where things go from here.

○ ○ ○

CHAPTER 1

THE STAND-UP PHILOSOPHER

The softly spoken, young, black, South African talk-show host is reading his teleprompter, and is about to mispronounce the word "philosopher." With an endearingly deferential demeanor, he looks into the camera and introduces me enthusiastically to his audience throughout the African continent:

"Today I am privileged to have with me Timothy Freke . . . a best-selling author and world-famous *falafel.*"

I smile to myself as I think about my adventures as a "famous falafel," which have taken me all over the world, sharing some extra-ordinary ideas with all kinds of people.

I am doing this television interview to promote my "stand-up philosophy" tour of South Africa, during which I've performed for kids at a township school, an elite gathering of business CEOs in a high-tech conference suite, intellectuals and passersby in a coffeehouse in a Johannesburg mall, and earnest spiritual seekers at a New Age festival. And wherever I go, my message is essentially the same:

It is possible to experience an ultraconscious state, which I call being "deep awake," in which we see that, although we seem to be separate individuals, in reality we are one. And this realization is accompanied by an awesome experience I call "big love," because when we know that we are one with all, we find ourselves in love with all.

Becoming deep awake leads to a new way of life that I call "lucid living." When we live lucidly, our everyday experience of life is transformed in surprising ways, unimaginable in the familiar waking state. The numbness we call "normality" dissipates like fog, and we become overwhelmed with wonder at the breathtaking magnificence of the universe. Our ordinary lives are transformed into an exhilarating love affair with the mystery of the moment.

This can all sound pretty outlandish, but I don't ask people to just believe what I say. As a philosopher, I am a devotee of doubt. Everyone has a built-in "bullshit detector," and I always suggest that my audience keep it on at all times, and check out everything I suggest in their own experience.

The ideas I talk about point to a state of consciousness that is available to everyone. My job is to help people experience the reality of lucid living for themselves. It's an unusual way to make a living, but if you've managed to survive school with a surname pronounced "freak," you're up for anything!

The Gift of the Present

The interview is going well. The charming talk-show host reverentially turns to the African professor who is joining us for this discussion to ask for his reactions to my books. He is smartly attired in traditional dress and clearly held in high regard as a spokesperson for the emerging African self-confidence. I'm surprised that he has even heard of me, let alone has an opinion about my work.

I sit in a state of pleased embarrassment as he enthuses at length about the importance of my ideas for Africans, saying that they reawaken an indigenous understanding that is in danger of being lost. He ends by boldly proclaiming that I'm a "gift" to Africa. Our host is clearly moved as he announces portentously, "You have been given a new name. Henceforth you will be known as 'Timothy "Gift" Freke.'"

I feel so honored that I'm lost for words. Where else but Africa could I be renamed live on TV? It feels good to be appreciated. I wish we would all spend more time appreciating each other. But I also know that I am not the real "gift" that has touched my new African friends so deeply. The gift is the state of deep awake, which arises when we enter the mystery of the moment. And while this is something I can point to, ultimately it's something we must each experience for ourselves.

Ever since I spontaneously experienced the deep awake state for the first time, when I was 12 years old, I've felt passionately driven to share this ecstatic experience with others. And I soon discovered that when I was deep awake, others started waking up around me, because states of consciousness are catching.

My life has been an adventure of awakening. I've immersed myself in the world's spiritual traditions, which opened my mind. I've studied academic philosophy, which sharpened my mind. I've spent years in meditative retreat, which calmed my mind. And I've experimented with psychedelic drugs and shamanic power-plants, which blew my mind.

I've practiced various spiritual techniques, which transformed my state of consciousness. I've explored the murky depths of my unconscious neuroses, which punctured my pride. I've worked with the dying, which opened my heart. And I've sat at the feet of charismatic gurus, who emptied my wallet.

In my 30s and 40s, I found myself writing a number of books on the major spiritual traditions of the world—Hinduism, Buddhism, Gnostic Christianity, Islamic Sufism, Shamanism, Hermeticism, Zen, Taoism, ancient Paganism—showing that they are all essentially concerned with helping us become deep awake. And so I have become an "authority" on world spirituality . . . at least, that's what it says on the back of my books!

But the truth is, I don't see myself as an "authority" figure at all. I certainly have no interest in setting myself up as some sort of "spiritual teacher," dispensing wisdom from a supposed exalted state that ordinary folk can't hope to emulate. I'm really turned off by all that elitist hype. I'm simply a passionate explorer of the mysteries of existence, reporting back from my expeditions into the uncharted regions of consciousness, to offer a road map to my fellow explorers who fancy making the trip themselves.

It was to avoid the role of "spiritual teacher" that I started calling myself a "stand-up philosopher." I see myself as reinvigorating the ancient tradition in which philosophers were traveling performers who wandered from place to place, challenging people's "common-sense" assumptions and opening their minds to new ways of seeing the world. I want to make philosophy fashionable again, so people care about what they think as much as they do about how they look.

Today philosophy is often dismissed as abstract and irrelevant, but the opposite is true. Changing the way we think transforms our experience of living. If we put up with a shallow, uninspiring understanding of what it is to be alive, we end up living shallow, uninspired lives. We exist on the surface of things, oblivious to the mysterious depths. We become members of the semiconscious crowd, rushing around as if there were no more to existence than making a living and not thinking about dying. We smother our need for meaning by willingly offering ourselves up to be mesmerized by the mass media into the collective coma we mistake for reality. Until eventually, stupefied by trivia, we become bored and tired of life.

Philosophy is usually perceived as a grown-up, serious business, but actually it is extremely childlike and playful. It's children, after all, who instinctively pose the big philosophical questions about life that grown-ups avoid asking. We adults enjoy being around happy children because it awakens memories of how we used to feel when being alive was a thrilling adventure, not a tiresome routine. It reminds us of a time when each day was a gift to be enjoyed, not a grind to be endured. As a stand-up philosopher, it's my job to be childlike enough to playfully question the close-mindedness that we confuse with maturity. And to suggest a new understanding of life that can wake us up to the real world of magic, mystery, and miracles.

Lucid Dreaming and Lucid Living

It's the evening after my unusual TV interview, and life is as unpredictable as ever. Tonight I'm performing alongside a collective of African poets, singers, and storytellers in Johannesburg. As I walk onstage, I catch a glimpse of my image in a mirror. Converging on my eyes are bold black-and-white lines of makeup.

Earlier this evening I was taken to a colorful traditional restaurant, where the waitress unexpectedly painted my face. And that's why I now find myself performing philosophy in downtown "Jo'Burg" looking more like a warrior than a wordsmith. Philosophy has such a reputation for being dull and dusty, I've often fantasized about adding some glamour to my stand-up-philosophy gigs by mischievously wearing a little makeup. It's strange how things work out.

I begin by sharing my recent "falafel" experience, which gets a laugh. Then I roam around the stage animatedly, which raises the energy, while I introduce myself, talk about my approach to philosophy, and crack some jokes. Now I feel ready to begin exploring the big questions that fascinate me. I'm going to take this part of the show real slow, because I want to share some challenging ideas. So I become very still, and the audience becomes alert and concentrated. Then I jump in with the simplest and deepest question I know:

"What is life? What is this strange flow of shapes and colors and sounds and thoughts that we're experiencing? What is this moment *right now?*

"I want to make an outrageous suggestion . . .

"Things are not what they seem to be, and you're not who you think you are . . . because life is like a dream and you are the dreamer.

"I want to suggest that normally we're pretty unconscious, but it's possible to experience an ultraconscious state of being deep awake, in which we realize that life is like a dream. I'm not offering this as an abstract possibility. I'm hanging out in this state right now, and simply describing what I'm experiencing.

"And it seems to me that the deep awake state is similar to lucid dreaming, only it's happening while I'm awake. That's why I call it 'lucid living.'

"You may have had a lucid dream at some time. Lucid dreaming is dreaming consciously. Normally we're unconsciously engrossed in our dreams. But occasionally we become more conscious. The dream continues, but we know that we're dreaming.

"I'm experiencing something similar now. I'm deep awake and living lucidly, because I'm conscious that life is like a dream.

"When I live lucidly, it profoundly changes my understanding of who I am, since I see that essentially there is one primal awareness dreaming itself to be everyone and everything.

"I am the primal awareness imagining itself to be 'Tim.' You are the primal awareness imagining itself to be 'you.' We appear to be separate individuals, but essentially there is one of us.

"This is the perennial message at the heart of all spiritual traditions, and it is something you can know for yourself if you carefully examine your experience of the present moment. So let's do that together now . . ."

The New Edge Tribe

The gig has gone well, and the room is buzzing with big love. My provocative ideas and the African artists' songs and poems have harmonized beautifully, creating a feeling of deep communion and ecstatic vision. It always blows me away how intoxicatingly sweet it is

when we connect through the illusion of separateness that seems to
divide us.

I'm winding down, drinking a beer with some of the other performers, when a young black singer with the most penetrating eyes
takes me by the hand. He looks at me intensely and tells me sol-
emnly:

> "Although our skin is of a different color and we were born
> into different cultures, we come from the same tribe."

I can't tell you how good this feels for a middle-aged, middle-
class, white boy from affluent England.

The striking young singer's words reverberate in my mind because
I can see that he's right. There's a new tribe arising to which we both
belong. A tribe of people drawn together by choice, not circumstance.
A tribe united not by race or geography or history, but by a shared
experience of the new consciousness that is emerging at the cutting
edge of evolution. A tribe that has rejected the old idea of "us and
them" and replaced it with the profound realization that there is only
"us." A tribe that knows we are all one.

When I first started the work of waking people up to oneness, I
found that only a handful of individuals seemed open to such a radical message. But over the years I've seen this change. Now I find that
more and more men and women come up to me after my presentations and say things like:

> "Thank you for helping me understand so clearly what I've
> been experiencing in my own life but couldn't put into
> words."

And that's when it hits me: I have to write a philosophy book that
can wake us up, designed for the new tribe emerging at the cutting
edge of evolution. It will be the fruition of more than three decades
of living on the edge, in which I have become familiar with the deep
awake state and have developed simple ways of helping people live
lucidly.

I've written a lot of books already, but this one will be different. I want to make my ideas even more accessible and relevant. I need to show that waking up to oneness and big love is a real experience that transforms everyday life. The problem is that writing about waking up is like explaining a joke, when what I really want is people to get the joke and fall over laughing.

How can I take others to the deep awake state? Perhaps by authentically recounting my own experiences and what they have taught me? My life is what I have to offer others. Previously I've written about philosophical ideas, but now the time has come to explore these ideas in a more personal book. I could write it as a series of anecdotal vignettes, like a postmodern film, and let the reader piece the story line together scene by scene.

Enlightenment and Enlivenment

I've found a quiet spot to drink my beer and think about our collective awakening. Mystics have been talking about the deep awake state for centuries. But I have a strong sense that the time has finally come to take the wisdom of oneness out of the mystical ghetto and into mainstream culture. And to do this we need ways of communicating timeless teachings that are designed for the 21st century. Everything must evolve . . . including our understanding of the deep awake state.

Although I've been heavily influenced by my studies of spirituality, these days I find most established spiritual traditions to be weighed down by religious ways of thinking that are well past their sell-by date. In their day, traditional forms of spirituality were dangerously radical, but now they've become safely conservative. They can't free us from the past because they *are* the past. We need something fresh to take us over the new edge.

In particular, I don't like it when traditional forms of spirituality present the deep awake state as the preserve of an "enlightened" elite, because it seems to me it's a natural state available to all. It's not a "spiritual Oscar" awarded to those fanatically devoted to intense practices. Indeed, the whole idea of spiritual "discipline" makes waking up sound about as much fun as going to the dentist.

I also have problems with any puritanical rejection of sexuality, intoxication, and pleasure in general. When the world is described as "the devil's playground," this just makes it sound more attractive to me. In my experience, life on the new edge is wickedly playful.

I want a spirituality that's passionate about life. After all, the delights of this world are so rich and various that it seems criminal not to appreciate them. Just drinking this beer . . . the coolness, the bubbles, the feeling of refreshment . . . it's all so intensely pleasurable when I really enter into my sensations. That has to be a good thing!

In my experience, being deep awake is both a state of transcendental enlightenment and embodied *enlivenment*. It's knowing that all is one and enjoying the play of separateness from that perspective. And this is why I find the concept of "lucid living" so powerful. When I dream lucidly, the dream doesn't end—I simply start to dream consciously. In the same way, when I live lucidly, the life-dream doesn't stop, I simply start to live more consciously. And this is the secret to really enjoying the life-dream.

Spiritual Junk Food

I'm taking a night flight back to the U.K. The cabin lights are off and I'm sitting with my eyes closed, allowing my imagination to roam. Right now I'm considering a question that is troubling me. Regardless of age, class, or race, there is a growing body of us who are in the process of becoming deep awake, yet our numbers are still extremely small. Why doesn't everyone wake up? What is standing in the way?

I usually assume the problem is that we're just not ready to wake up. But maybe there's more to it than that? Perhaps the problem also lies with the state of modern spirituality? Spirituality has the role of waking us up, but is it up to the job?

There's a gullibility that pervades modern spirituality. As a philosopher, this disturbs me because without rational doubt, we easily become lost in fantasy, rather than waking up to reality. Modern spirituality needs to consider what philosophers call "epistemology." Before we can say "what we know," we need to think about "how we know it."

Do we take channeled wisdom from the ascended masters residing in the Pleiades at face value? Or do we stop and ask ourselves, "How can I check if this is for real?" We need to keep an open mind and listen to our intuition, for life is strange and anything is possible. But we also need to be savvy and judicious.

Many people today, however, are consuming large amounts of spiritual junk food without chewing—so there's an epidemic of philosophical indigestion. We've become so transfixed with the mysteries of the crop circles and the crystal skulls that we're ignoring the real mystery . . . which is that we exist and don't know what to do about it!

And here's another thing that bothers me. I hate all the sanctimonious seriousness and saccharine niceness so often associated with being "spiritual." It gets in the way of our being authentic with each other. Some of the new "gurus" are so safely bland it's like listening to elevator music. That's not going to enliven us. It's going to put us to sleep in a comfortable spiritual cocoon.

For me, the real heroes of the new edge of evolution are radically real people like the late Bill Hicks . . . a comic genius who took us to big love via his own unique brand of taboo-breaking, consciousness-raising, misanthropic humor. Even though Bill Hicks is dead now, if I had the choice of hanging out with him or Swami Blandananda, it would be no contest.

Damn it! I think I'm beginning to become a channel myself. I can hear Bill's manic Texan drawl raving in my ears:

"Listen up! I've got some really good news! Everything is okay!

"Being alive is weird and scary and never really makes sense, but that's all right because life is like a dream . . . so there's nothing to be alarmed about . . . it all turns out all right in the end . . . because when you die in a dream, you wake up.

"But before you bow out, why not enjoy the show . . . because it's a thrilling roller coaster of a ride . . . and when you stop worrying about falling off, you can just throw your hands up in the air and yell 'Bring it on!' . . . as you career through the highs and lows of the ever-changing moment . . . toward the sign marked 'exit.'

"Heh! I know what I'm talking about because *I'm dead!* The way to enjoy the trip is to lighten up, not tighten up!

"If you take things too seriously, you'll be popping Prozac just to cope with the anxiety . . . and when 'numb' becomes 'normal,' every day will be a monotonous cycle of drudgery. Then you'll remember all the things you need to get done . . . but forget the most important thing about life . . . and that's this . . .

"IT'S HAPPENING RIGHT NOW AND IT'S TOTALLY AWESOME!"

For some reason the cabin lights have just gone on, and I'm conscious that I've been ranting to myself. It's just an expression of my frustration with the state of modern spirituality. I'm really a "love junkie" who hates being critical, so I feel embarrassed by my bombast . . . although no one was listening except me.

Actually, of course, there's room for a whole spectrum of approaches to waking up. Spirituality, like music, is a matter of taste. Some people like classical spirituality and others like pop. I get impatient with both, because I want things to be accessible without sacrificing depth. But it's no good just carping on about what I *don't* like. I need to offer my own idiosyncratic approach as another option.

That's what I'll do in my new book. And if spirituality *were* music, I'd like it to combine the irreverent iconoclasm of rock 'n' roll, the sophistication of acid jazz, the clarity of minimalist glitch, the big heart of old-school soul, the infectious drive of funky breakbeat . . . and, in an ideal world, the mass appeal of big-hit bubblegum!

Then the flight attendant says, "Please fasten your safety belts; we're experiencing turbulence." And this brings my attention to how uncomfortably narrow my seat is, and how much I wish the chunky guy next to me wouldn't keep prodding me with his elbow . . . which makes me question my aspirations. Maybe I should just go for spiritual bubblegum and the big bucks? Because in the future, I need to be traveling first class.

Coming Home

My little girl won't stop hugging me. My teenage son is also pleased to see me, although he's less inclined to show it demonstratively. My wife, Debbie, is looking even more gorgeous than I remembered. It's good to be back home from South Africa to life as a family man. I need time off from presenting myself as the fascinating thinker on TV and the charismatic performer onstage. Now I need to worry about paying the bills and fixing the dishwasher.

There was a time when such mundane concerns were a burden to me because they seemed so trivial compared to exploring the mysteries of existence. And yet the strange thing is that the more I've experienced the ecstatic joy of being deep awake, the more I've come to appreciate the miracle of every moment. The more I've recognized that all is one, the more I've fallen in love with this separate individual named "Tim" . . . and his extraordinarily ordinary life.

CHAPTER 2

THE MYSTERY
OF THE MOMENT

I'm sitting with my dog on a quiet hill overlooking my small hometown and all of its insignificant busyness. I'm 12 years old, and I'm thinking about some big questions that fascinate me: *Why are we here? What's the purpose of life? What happens after death? What should I do with my life? Why is there so much suffering in the world? How can I be truly happy? How can I really help others?*

I'm convinced that I've been born on the wrong planet because I clearly don't belong here. Being alive is so profoundly strange, yet the grown-ups around me seem to just take everything for granted. It's as if they've fallen into some sort of coma and don't notice that they're alive. Or perhaps they've secretly agreed never to talk about the big questions of life, but to anesthetize themselves with trivia.

Everyone goes about their daily business as if they know exactly what life is all about. But I can see that no one's really got a clue as to what's going on. Most people just go along with whatever ideas are currently in vogue, whether they're about makeup, music, or the nature of reality. Something inside of me rages against their inane, unquestioning, "commonsense" approach to life. I refuse to believe that my purpose in this extravagant universe could be to climb a career ladder, buy a house, and get a pension plan. Life is too important to waste just making money and acquiring things. Life is like an enormous question that demands an answer.

And then, unexpectedly and inexplicably, it happens. . . .

My train of thought jolts to a halt, and the whole world starts vibrating, sending seismic shudders through my soul. I feel as if the top of my head has just come off and the sky has poured in. I'm overwhelmed by awesome, unfathomable, breathtaking mystery. I don't know anything. *Nobody* knows anything. Life is a miracle of such enormous proportions that the mind can't possibly comprehend it.

I seem to have inexplicably slipped into another reality in which the colors are brighter and the birds sing symphonies. I'm immersed in wonder. I feel a bizarre sense of oneness with everything around me, as if I'm the universe looking at itself, amazed by its own beauty. I'm utterly happy for no reason at all. I feel certain beyond doubt of the goodness of all that is.

The humdrum world has peeled away like a superficial veneer, revealing a secret garden that I've always suspected was close by. I know this place. It feels like home. But how can it be so familiar when it's unlike anything I've ever experienced? I have no idea what is happening to me. But I know that my life will never be the same again. And I know that the answer I'm searching for so desperately is not a clever theory about life. It's this experience of wonder in which all of my questions dissolve.

And then there is sudden, deep silence. I'm consumed by the sensation of sinking, as if I'm being engulfed by an ocean of bliss. Spasms of relaxation ripple through my young body, and I feel embraced by such a love that tears of relief spring spontaneously to my eyes. The entire vast universe is pulsating with limitless love. It is held together by love. And I am that love. There is only love. I've been born to experience this moment.

A Journey of Awakening

It's Monday morning, and my wife and I have successfully nego-tiated getting our children off to school. Sleepy bodies have been washed, dressed, and filled with fuel for the day. The lost gym bag has been found. The pretense of having a sore throat has been seen through. The TV has been turned off, and the kids have been bundled out the door. Now I'm sitting in my spacious office at the end of our funky little garden, working on this book that you're reading.

I wanted to start by telling you about my first deep awake experi-ence as a boy because it has been the seed from which my life has grown. I don't know how long that experience lasted, since it had a timeless quality, but it probably wasn't long. I eventually made my way down the hill, back to my life as a kid in small-town England. But something had changed.

I was now on a quest to understand what had happened to me so that I could find a way back to the secret garden. I'd embarked on a journey of awakening, which is still continuing today. And throughout this journey, I've found myself waking up to oneness and big love again and again, often at the most unexpected times. It's a state I've come to know well and return to regularly.

In this book I'm going to share some of my deep awake experi-ences with you, along with what they have taught me. I'll begin by taking you progressively deeper into the experience of lucid living so that you'll be able to taste the bliss of big love for yourself. Then we'll explore how, when we're in this ultraconscious state, everyday life becomes transformed into a wonderful adventure full of meaning, miracles, and magic. Finally, I'm going to help you avoid some com-mon spiritual misunderstandings that can prevent you from waking up, offer you a radically new understanding of the nature of death, and explore how we can co-create a deep awake world. So I think you'll find that it's gonna be an exciting trip!

The philosophy I'm going to share with you is the mystical heart of spirituality, so it's very deep and powerfully transformative. I've done all I can to make these ideas as accessible as possible, but they're so different from our so-called commonsense view of life that they may well seem strange at first. Be patient with yourself if you find some parts of this book easier to follow than others. And stay open to the possibility that ideas that don't resonate with you at first may make more sense as we go along.

Throughout the book, I'll suggest that you experiment with various wake-up techniques so that you go beyond the ideas to the actual experience of being deep awake. We all have different temperaments, so some of the wake-up techniques I suggest may work well for you, but other techniques may not. That's okay. Just focus on what works for you.

Some of the deep awake experiences I'm going to relate are pretty dramatic, but it might not be like that in your experience. My own journey has been marked by sudden bursts of greater consciousness and new insights. But I know plenty of very awake people whose journeys have been characterized by gentle development.

This book is about waking up and living lucidly, but trying to wake up is like trying to fall in love—it's a natural process that happens when it happens. Even so, there are things we can do to create the space for a natural awakening to occur.

We can be authentically open to the possibility of experiencing a new state of consciousness. We can change our understanding of life and look at reality with new eyes. And we can explore the present moment using simple wake-up techniques. This book will help you do these things. And my greatest hope is that when our time together comes to an end, you'll find yourself living lucidly.

The Ever-Present Mystery

When I woke up as a 12-year-old, I had no idea why my state of consciousness had changed so unexpectedly. Looking back, however, I can see that I'd focused so intensely on how strange life seemed to me that it catapulted me into the mystery. And ever since, I've found that when I focus my attention on how mysterious existence is, my state of consciousness changes and I start to wake up. In my experience, the mystery of this moment is an open doorway to the deep awake state—and we can step through whenever we like.

The problem is that normally we're so unconscious that we don't even notice the mystery, even though it actually is utterly obvious. Right now, for instance, I'm sitting before my computer screen, staring at this jumble of words. In many ways it's an ordinary day for Tim the author, because I've done this countless times before. There's nothing strange about it. And yet, when I really pay attention to what's happening, I see that it's profoundly mysterious.

Thoughts are arising in my consciousness, but what is consciousness exactly? And what is a "thought"? And where do they keep coming from? I'm told that it's something to do with the porridge in my head, where millions of neurons are firing away, encoding my ideas into language. And then I'm encoding these words into symbolic marks on the page. And you're looking at these marks, which the porridge in *your* head is decoding back into words, so *my* thoughts are arising in *your* consciousness. Through this incredible play of forms, two conscious beings are connecting with each other. How amazing!

Now I'm noticing my hands typing on the keyboard. They feel so solid and real. Yet the physicists I hang out with tell me that my body is mostly empty space. Right now there are zillions of cosmic particles passing straight through my body, through the earth, and out the other side without touching anything. I'm mostly nothing! It's impossible to get my head around that.

The human predicament is so astonishingly strange it amazes me that we aren't in a permanent state of confusion. Here we are . . . clever monkeys clinging to a lump of rock, hurtling around a giant nuclear-power station in the sky, in a solar system of such enormous proportions that to imagine it makes our brains go *pop!* And that's just our solar system, since there are more than 100 billion stars! And that's just in our galaxy, since there more than 100 billion galaxies!

It makes me laugh when TV documentaries say that scientists are on the verge of explaining the universe, as if to assure us that someone somewhere knows what's going on. But the truth is that science has simply confounded the problem. Life looks even weirder now than it did before. In the past, we accepted things as they seemed to be . . . the earth was flat, the sky was up, solid objects were solid objects. Science has presented us with a far stranger world that undermines all of these commonsense assumptions. It has led us deeper into the mystery, as great scientists such as Newton and Einstein fully recognized.

Recently, I read in a scientific journal that only 4 percent of the universe is made of matter as we know it. The other 96 percent is . . . who knows what?! In light of this, it seems to me that anyone who is certain that they know what life's about is clearly mad . . . and dangerous.

The more I learn, the more bizarre life becomes. After more than three decades of exploration, all I really know is what I discovered when I unexpectedly entered the deep awake state as a boy: *Life is a mystery.* And if you dive deeply into the mystery, you'll be *so* pleased that you did, because this is the most awesome experience possible.

A Conceptual Matrix

This is very cool. I'm performing at an unusual London nightclub called "OneTaste," which is dedicated to entertainment that alters consciousness. I'm on the bill with some excellent poets and singers. The audience of mainly young people is sitting around small, dimly lit tables; and the atmosphere is electric. I pause for as long as I dare to allow the crowd to come into stillness . . . and then I begin:

> "I was reading the evolutionary biologist Richard Dawkins recently, and he was explaining that our brains construct a model of the world that we move around in, which he describes as 'a kind of virtual-reality simulation of the world.'

> "Isn't that interesting? It's just like in *The Matrix,* except we're not living in a computer-generated reality; we're inhabiting a world constructed from ideas. We're living in a conceptual matrix created by the mind, which helps us understand the awesome mystery of existence."

Then I announce with a flourish:

"Tonight, ladies and gentlemen, I want to set us free from our conceptual incarceration so that we can experience together the transformation in consciousness that occurs when we step out of the matrix and into the mystery. And I'm going to do this by performing an amazing magic trick."

I take off my watch, hold it up before the crowd, and announce:

"I'm going to make this watch disappear."

Then, backpedaling on this audacious claim, I explain,

"Actually, I'm going to show you how to make the watch disappear . . . using no more than the power of your imagination."

I wave the watch around dramatically and ask, "What do you see?" The audience kindly plays along by calling out "a watch."

"Okay. Now I want you to imagine that you don't come from this culture. You have been born in the deepest jungles of Borneo and don't know anything about Western civilization. And then you inexplicably find yourself here with this bald-headed man waving something in front of you."

I pause for people to attempt this impossible task, and then I ask,

"Do you see a watch now?"

The room is hushed in puzzled concentration for a moment and some voices call out, "No," so I continue,

"That's right. You only see a watch when you have the concept of 'watch.' If you came from the jungles of Borneo, you'd see whatever you could conceptualize. You might see 'leather' or 'bracelet' or 'round metal object,' but you wouldn't see 'watch.' Only if I explained to you the Western idea of time, how we measure it, and how we represent its passage with a clock would you see 'watch.'

- "We are conscious of what we can conceptualize. As I look around me now, I see that I have a concept for everything I'm conscious of . . . 'stage' . . . 'lights' . . . 'microphone' . . . 'people' . . . 'Tim' . . . everything! Is it like that for you, too? Have a look for yourself . . ."

Several people in the audience are smiling broadly, which is always a sign that they can see what I'm saying. It can be pretty bizarre when they really start to get it, so I explain,

"We're experiencing this moment through a filter of concepts. We're living in our ideas. We're telling ourselves a story about who we are and what life is, and we're confusing this story with reality. But the story is not reality. Reality is the mystery of existence that exists before all of our ideas about reality.

"We've become bamboozled by our beliefs, and this has blinded us to the primal mystery. We've become so engrossed with our stories that we've lost the plot. We're eating the menu, not the meal, and that's why life can taste so bland."

The room is very still now, and I can see from their faces that some people are experiencing the strange reality shift that philosophy can induce. Then I ask,

"What happens if we put aside our ideas for a moment and enter a profound state of not knowing? What happens if we step out of confines of the conceptual mind into the spacious openness of the mystery?" *I'm free.*

Loving Life or Just Getting on with It

I'm drinking a cappuccino at a pavement café and people watching. It's a favorite pastime of mine because I can see that everyone is living in a story about who he or she is and what life is.

That guy over there with the briefcase looks like he lives in a world in which succeeding is what matters . . . although he's secretly worried that he might be a loser. The pretty young woman reading the magazine hasn't decided who she is yet . . . but she's considering a story that revolves around becoming a model with enormous breasts. The nervous father pushing the stroller, on the other hand, looks like he's just had his whole story turned upside down . . . but he seems to be enjoying it.

We all live in a story. Mine is the story of "Tim" . . . the philosopher plumbing the depths of life . . . the father trying to support a family . . . the author attempting to write a bestseller. I can't tell you how much I love my story. But sometimes I become so lost in my dramas that I don't notice the underlying mystery of existence. And then life starts to go dead on me.

It's like when a romantic relationship loses its magic.

Look at that young couple window-shopping—right now they're so in love. You know what it's like. You meet someone and they seem so amazing. They're a mystery to you, and you're a mystery to them. And when you meet in that mystery, you say that you're in love with each other. It feels as if you're walking on sunshine and life is sweet. But as time goes by, things usually change.

And that, I'm guessing, is exactly what's happened to the middle-aged woman arguing with her husband at the table opposite from mine. He used to see her as a sublime mystery, but over the years he's adopted a lot of limiting ideas about her. Now he's put her into a conceptual box, so she feels cramped and confined. He can no longer see the mystery she really is because he's relating to an *idea* of who she is. This is preventing them from authentically connecting, so the magic has gone from their relationship. When that happens, we say that we've fallen out of love . . . which is exactly right.

I find that it's the same with life. When I put the mystery of existence into a conceptual box, the magic goes. I stop loving my life and I start just getting on with it. But when I step out of my story into the mystery, it's as if I've suddenly remembered that I'm alive again, and I find myself falling in love with everything and everyone.

I'm conscious of the mystery now, and all of my superficial judgments are dissolving. I love the middle-aged woman for giving her husband a hard time, since she so much wants them to be together in the mystery again. I love the new father for embracing a change of direction that fills him with fear of the future. I love the businessman for his ambition and the pretty young woman for her naïveté. Who knows where their strange lives will lead? Maybe to the ever-present mystery of this moment?

The Importance of the Story

It's been a very special night. Sharing my philosophy at the One-Taste club has allowed everyone present to taste the oneness together. Now I'm having fun taking questions from the audience. A lot of people seem really attracted to the ideas I've been sharing. But now a sharply dressed man at the back is about to speak, and I can see from his expression that he's skeptical:

> "This notion that I can just let go of my story and step into the mystery is utter nonsense. If I did let go of my story, I'd be an amnesiac, for goodness' sake. I wouldn't know where I am or how to get home. I wouldn't be deep awake; I'd be profoundly lost."

I feel resistance to his comment in the room because we've been playing in the mystery for some time, and most people are reluctant to go back to critical thinking quite yet. But I'm happy for him to push me, because doubt makes us more conscious, so I reply:

"Please don't misunderstand me. I'm not saying that we should abandon our stories about life because, as you say, this would leave us utterly disoriented.

"Actually, we're only conscious at all because we're discriminating everything with concepts. Without concepts we wouldn't differentiate individual things in the amorphous oneness of 'what-is.'

"Ideas are great. I love them. But that doesn't mean we have to be so mesmerized by our ideas that we miss the mystery. We need a story to help us navigate our lives. But it's possible to *also* see beyond the story to the mystery. It's not either/or . . . it's both/and.

"The mystery and the story are polarities that coexist in the moment, and we need to be conscious of both. As I'm speaking to you, I'm conscious of the mystery, but I'm also conscious of the story of Tim. If I wasn't, I wouldn't be able to engage in this stimulating conversation."

The man at the back still looks uneasy and needs to push me harder, so he continues,

"I have to say that my experience of the mystery hasn't been good. A few years ago I really lost the plot in my story, and it took me to the edge of a mental breakdown. Before this happened, I had a strong sense of my own identity and where I was going in life. Then suddenly nothing made sense, and I felt totally lost. Without my story, life seemed meaningless, and I became depressed. I wouldn't recommend that to anyone."

Now we're getting somewhere. He's not questioning me out of intellectual curiosity. This really matters to him, so I'm careful with my response:

"I've also experienced my story breaking down so that I was unable to make sense of my life. I know it's not a good place to be, which is why I'm not recommending that you abandon your story and just be conscious of the mystery.

"In my case, what happened was this. I became so engrossed in my story that I was <u>unconscious of the mystery</u>, which meant that I <u>no longer felt truly alive</u>. Eventually I felt so confined by the story that I detonated the whole thing to set myself free. I unconsciously catapulted myself into the state of 'not-knowing.' And as I didn't know what was happening, I panicked. This made me cling desperately to the remnants of my story, but it just wasn't working anymore. So I started drowning in meaninglessness.

"However, there's nothing so bad that good can't come from it. And there was a positive side to this experience because when the dust settled, my story came back together . . . but in a new way. I had a deeper understanding of Tim and his world. The <u>breakdown</u> became a <u>breakthrough</u>.

"From what I hear, many of us have experienced something like this. In some cases, the breakdown can be precipitated by some unpleasant event that our story is just not big enough to make meaningful. And in extreme cases, it's impossible to put things back together without professional assistance. But for most of us, it's a phase on the journey of awakening that, in retrospect, was necessary and even benign. . . . Was it like this in your experience?"

He thinks about this for a while and then replies,

"I guess it was. Things have moved on. Life has gotten better."

I continue,

"So here's the thing. We don't need to have a breakdown to have a breakthrough. We don't need to wait until we're so entrenched in our story that the only way out is through some sort of violent psychological revolution. We can be conscious of the mystery right now, without dismantling our story. And then there's room for the story to naturally evolve and deepen, since we can see new possibilities all the time."

Now he's looking more relaxed and his tone of voice softens,

"I can see that. My story has evolved listening to you this evening. And it's been a painless experience . . . most of the time."

We both laugh, and so does the audience. Then I say,

"Well, I'm glad about that because, as a philosopher, I'm in the business of changing people's stories. And if we must have a story, then it seems to me that we'd better make it a good one.

"Superficial stories lead to superficial lives. Deep ideas allow deep experiences. Philosophy is about finding the best story possible. And for me, that means a story that includes the possibility of becoming deep awake.

"The paradox of our predicament is that to wake up, we need to see beyond our story to the mystery. But we also need a story to become deep awake. It's much more difficult to wake up when your story of life excludes this possibility.

"And if you were lucky enough to stumble upon the deep awake state, like I did as a boy, you wouldn't know how to get back there, because your story will have nothing to say about this.

"I've spent my whole life working up a story about life that can help me become deep awake."

The man at the back looks genuinely intrigued, so I add with a cheeky grin,

"I'm going to explore this story in the new book I'm writing at the moment. Maybe you should preorder a copy?"

He smiles back playfully and says,

"I can't tell if that was an answer or a sales pitch."

And that makes the crowd clap, because my audiences tend to appreciate smart-assed mavericks.

Consider the Obvious

I'm hanging out in the deep awake state right now, and I'd love for you to join me. All you need to do is become conscious of the mystery of the moment. This doesn't require you to abandon your story, only for you to place it to one side for a while and focus your attention on the most obvious thing about your predicament . . . that it's profoundly enigmatic.

You can do this now by focusing on the feeling that there is much more to life than you understand. Most people relegate this feeling of uncertainty to the background of the mind, where it can be conveniently ignored. But if you bring it into the foreground of your attention, something interesting will start to happen to your state of consciousness.

Sometimes it can feel frightening to dive into the mystery. We want to hold on to something because we associate not being certain about things with feeling confused and anxious. But dissolving into the mystery is actually an experience of ecstatic liberation, not worried perplexity.

It can be terrifying when we hover nervously on the outskirts of the mystery, but when we unconditionally let go into the mystery, there's nothing to fear. When we finally recognize that we truly know nothing, there is an exhilarating feeling of freedom and an overwhelming sense of wonder.

The mystery of life is so utterly obvious that it's astonishing we miss it so much of the time. We are like fish not noticing water. We are conscious of the eddies in the flow and the changes in temperature, but we don't see that it's all water. Normally we're so engrossed with our stories about life that we miss the ever-present mystery. But as soon as we step out of our story . . . there it is in all of its unfathomable glory.

Throughout my life, I've found that simply becoming conscious of the mystery wakes me up. The trick is to recognize when I've become lost in the story of Tim. The telltale clues are that I've become certain about things and overly anxious . . . and that I've lost my sense of humor. Then I simply step out of my story and into the mystery of the moment. I remember that I'm alive and how awesome that is.

When I see beyond my ideas about life, there's a wonderful feeling of oneness with all that is, since it's only my concepts that make me see *me included* things as separate. And when I know that essentially all is one, I find myself in love with life, because love is how oneness feels. So when I bring my attention back to the dramas I'm confronting, I see things through new eyes. And the more I hang out in the mystery, the easier it becomes to wake up the next time I'm lost in the story of Tim.

○ ○ ○

CHAPTER 3

THE BREATH OF LIFE

It's a dull, overcast day, and I'm sitting in a coffeehouse talking philosophy with my fellow student Anthony Taylor. I love his company because he combines a penetrating mind with a kind heart and calming presence. In the unimagined future, Anthony will go on to become the Director of the Alliance for Lucid Living, an organization designed to promote our collective awakening. But right now we are still in our early 20s. And it's the final year of our studies at the University of Bristol before we earn our BA degrees in Western philosophy.

I've thrown myself passionately into my studies, but I've also become increasingly disillusioned with academic philosophy, which seems dry and abstract, not remotely "life changing." But at least I've learned how to doubt deeply and think clearly. Maybe *too* clearly, because I've become a bit of a philosophical buccaneer who enjoys demolishing other people's opinions with a flourish of my sharp intellect.

For some time I've been so focused on my mental development that I haven't given much attention to being deep awake. Then a few weeks ago, something strange spontaneously started happening. I was sitting at my desk in my apartment writing an essay on existentialism, when I had the disquieting feeling of a vast emptiness opening up before me and inviting me into it. Intuitively, I knew that I should let go into the emptiness, but I was simply too scared to do so.

Over the course of the next few days, this happened a few times, and each time I held out. Now I'm sitting drinking coffee in this busy little café and it's happening again. It may be because I'm with Anthony, but this time I don't feel frightened. So I take him by the hands and interrupt our conversation, saying:

"Something weird is happening, Tony. Look out for me because I'm going to let go into it."

Anthony is intrigued and asks me to describe what I'm experiencing. I'm going to find this difficult, but I'll give it a go . . .

"My body is starting to vibrate . . . and so is the café.

"Everything seems spacious and empty . . . if that makes any sense?

"Something is happening to my breath. And it feels delicious. It's as if the whole universe is breathing me.

"I've never noticed before how exquisite it is just to breathe. I feel consumed by the experience of breathing. And the more I let go into my breath, the more intensely alive I feel . . .

"This is awesome. I couldn't possibly want for any more than to be here breathing. I'm completely in love with this moment. There's so much love that it's utterly overwhelming. . . ."

I'm smiling manically as I look across at Anthony. I can see from his face that he's also beginning to enter the same amazing breath experience. States of consciousness are catching!

So we sit there for a while in the vibrating café, staring into each other's eyes and grinning like idiots, oblivious to the other coffee drinkers chatting around us. Then Anthony suggests,

"Let's go to Brandon Hill."

In that magical way that life works, when we step outside it's like a new day. The sun is shining in a clear blue sky. The colors are bright and the sounds are crisp. The world seems alive and wonderfully mysterious. I feel as if the life force that is breathing me is the same life force that is animating everything.

As we make our way up the grassy inclines of Brandon Hill, we are laughing uncontrollably like children. And all I can say over and over again is,

"This breath . . . this breath . . . this breath . . ."

At the top of the hill we sit together overlooking the sprawling metropolis of Bristol city, feeling a rich contentment that only the shared silence can express. Life is good. We are deep awake.

Proof for the Existence of God

I'm in a lecture on the philosophy of religion. The young woman who's speaking is exploring rational proofs for the existence of God, and I'm having real trouble containing my giggles, which keep slipping out and disturbing the lecture. The breath experience is happening again, and I feel constantly on the edge of laughter . . . for no particular reason.

My first breath experience lasted for a few hours, but three days later it came back. I was in a nightclub listening to an old American blues singer . . . with Anthony again. And this time the experience has continued. Whenever I pay attention to my breath, it feels exquisite, and I find myself sinking into the mystery of the moment. I'm totally present to the miracle of living.

This has been a blissful period in my life, which has made my academic studies seem rather silly. I came to university looking for intellectual answers, but now I've remembered what I discovered when I was 12. The real answer to my questions lies in a transformation of consciousness.

As soon as exams are over, I'm going to find a quiet place in the country where I can live a simple life and really explore what happens when I dive deeply into this breath experience. I've read so many books—I've had enough of words. Now I want to explore the silence and see what it can teach me.

Then the lecturer says something that makes me burst out laughing. She has just spent three-quarters of an hour expounding a traditional "proof" for the existence of God, and then demolished it completely in a couple of minutes. But this is completely missing the point. The existence of God isn't something you can *prove* with logical arguments. "God" is a word for the mysterious life force in everything. And I'm experiencing the reality of that all-embracing life force right now.

Enter There

It's a beautiful summer day, and I'm sitting in a meadow by a pretty pink cottage, where I've come for a year of meditative retreat after finishing my academic studies. During this time I've spent long periods focusing on my breath, and I've found that this brings me into the mystery of the moment, so I begin to experience the deep awake state.

Right now I'm paddling my feet in the stream that runs through the meadow. And I'm thinking about an old Zen story in which a student asks about enlightenment, and the master simply replies,

"Can you hear the sound of that babbling brook?

"Enter there."

I love this story because it offers such a simple way to wake up. And it's working for me because as I focus on the tinkling tones of the stream, my state of consciousness is changing and I'm sinking into the deep awake state.

I have discovered that when I focus on any of my sensations, this disengages my attention from my story, and I start to feel immersed in mystery. I usually choose to focus on my breath—since it's always there, I can pay attention to it whenever I want. And I find that it is very pleasurable to sink into my breath, which helps as I'm a big fan of pleasure.

The philosopher Epicurus suggested that we become more conscious of pleasure, seeking out simpler and simpler pleasures until we become conscious of the immense pleasure of simply being. That's how I use my breath. I witness the pleasure of breathing, and then I find myself bathing in the bliss of being.

As I sit here in the meadow, I'm conscious of the smooth sensuality of my breath. I'm conscious of the music of the running water. I'm conscious of being deep awake. And now . . . unfortunately . . . I'm also conscious of how much the sound of running water is making me want to pee, so I'm going to have to dash inside.

The Moment Is Enough

I wanted to tell you about my breath experience because I still find that focusing on my breath takes me into the mystery of the moment. I've been exploring this wake-up technique ever since my experience with Anthony in the coffeehouse. It's simple and powerful . . . and I recommend you try it.

After graduating from university, I stayed as a guest with the novices at a beautiful Franciscan friary, as it was the perfect place for a spiritual retreat. I'd previously run away to this friary after an argument with my father when I was 15, so I already knew the Guardian, Brother Bernard, who became a lifelong mentor and friend. During my time at the friary, I developed a reputation as the young student who was always in the chapel "praying." I'm sure I seemed very devout, but the truth was that all I wanted to do was focus on breathing, since it felt so amazing. There was nothing holy about it. I was just sinking into bliss, and I didn't want to stop.

For a while I considered becoming a friar. I still had a student apartment in Bristol, and I wondered what would happen if I simply never returned. I had visions of my belongings taunting me, saying, "But we're your things, you've got to come back for us." And I did go back. Not for my things . . . but because I knew I loved women too much to be celibate.

When I left the friary, I rented the little pink cottage by the meadow, and it became my sanctuary. I was known locally as "Tim of the meadows" . . . that odd guy who spends all of his time meditating and practicing Tai Chi Chuan, which my landlord called "that funny Chinese dancing." I had nothing. I lived frugally. I did very little. Yet I had never been happier.

I spent my first night there curled up in front of a log fire reading *The Way of Zen* by Alan Watts. In one passage he explained that waking up wasn't an idea you could understand by reading a book; it was something to experience. I spontaneously threw the book on the fire and settled down to meditate. And that's pretty much all I did for the next year.

During this time I found that entering my breath was like sinking into a warm bath, which dissolved away all of my worries and anxieties, leaving me in love with life. And I realized something hugely important, which has shaped the rest of my life . . . I can be perfectly content just to breathe.

I've found this extremely liberating, because it's freed me from the need to seek fulfillment through all of the "normal" channels . . . wealth, success, power, fame. I already have all I need, and no one can take it away from me. No matter what fate might befall me, I know that it's possible to sink into my breath and enter the mystery of the moment.

When I'm deep awake, the moment is enough. And when I'm not, there is always this underlying feeling of dissatisfaction, even if things are going well. The Buddha called this *dukkha* . . . the suffering that never leaves us when we are lost in separateness. In my experience, this primal discontent only subsides when I'm immersed in the mystery of the moment. Then I can accept things just as they are, and I become content for no reason.

Stuck in the Story

I'm having a bad day. The kids have been hyper, and Debbie is stressed out about work. Or maybe I'm the one who's hyper and stressed out about the new book I'm working on. I'm feeling decidedly stuck in the story of "Tim," and it seems painfully hypocritical to write about waking up.

I've gone for a walk in the local cemetery, as I sometimes do when I want some peace. No one here is too noisy. And they're way past being stressed out. So I sit down on a bench and try to become conscious of the mystery of the moment. But I keep going over the same worried thoughts in my head. This is getting me nowhere.

Time for a little trick to free up my attention and snap me out of my story, which I learned long ago in my 20s. If the mystery is too elusive for me to find today, I'll focus on something a lot more tangible.

I place my attention on the physical sensation of my breath entering and leaving my body.

My thoughts are still racing, but I continue to breathe slowly in and out. And as I do so, I feel my body start to relax.

Then as I fully enter the feeling of breathing, the quality of my breath becomes more sensual.

Just to breathe feels very good, and I'm pulled into the delicious richness of my sensations.

I am becoming one with my breath and in love with breathing.

Starved of my attention, my agitated thoughts begin to quiet down.

I feel clear and spacious . . . relaxed and alert.

I am conscious of the mystery of the moment.

I sit there for a while, quietly enjoying being and breathing, until I feel ready to engage with my everyday dramas again. And from the deep awake state, the challenges in the story of Tim now seem less daunting. In fact, I'm feeling positively inspired to go and work on the book, since all of this will be great material to use.

Then my eye catches the name on the gravestone in front of me. This guy was also named "Timothy," and he died when he was about my age. He was once breathing like I am now. Then one day he stopped breathing and was gone. I wonder how many times he breathed in and out, between his first inhalation and last exhalation? And this makes me intensely conscious of how precious it is to be alive . . . and how important it is to appreciate each breath.

Meditation

I've been sleeping and I'm just coming around, sitting up in bed with my legs crossed, slouched against the wall behind me. I had intended to meditate on my breath, but I must have drifted off. I used to be a "macho meditator" who gave himself a hard time when this happened. But I'm a chilled-out meditator now.

I even rather enjoy the nodding-off process. I watch with interest as I get sucked into my thoughts, which start to become dreams, and my head involuntarily drops forward as I fall unconscious. Then I wrench my attention out of the dream and deliberately become conscious, which feels like trying to pull my hand out of a jar of molasses.

At one time I would have called this a "bad meditation." But now I see it as a useful philosophical exercise because it strengthens up the psychological "muscles" I need to stay awake during my everyday life. I'm aware that a comparable process is happening all the time. I'm getting sucked into the dream of Tim and then pulling back my attention to the mystery of the moment.

Focusing on the breath is a wake-up technique found in all spiritual traditions. But I try not to see it as a "discipline," since that turns it from a pleasure into a chore. Like everything in life, it doesn't always work. For me, waking up is an adventure, and if it wasn't a challenge some of the time it wouldn't be much of an adventure. But I try not to set up the expectation that waking up must be some momentous struggle, because this just gets in the way of its happening naturally.

Anyway . . . the time has come to stop meditating . . . or should I say dozing? I've got things to do and I need to get out of bed. I'm feeling drowsy, so it takes me an effort to rise lethargically to my feet. But now that I'm standing, it's easy. I stay still for a while and think about this, as it's the same with becoming deep awake. Sometimes my story is so sticky that it takes an effort of will to free myself up. But when I'm deep awake and living lucidly, it's utterly effortless.

What Don't We Notice?

Focusing on the sensation of breathing is a simple way to dive deeply into the mystery of the moment. Normally we're so unconscious that we don't even notice the mystery, even though it's actually utterly obvious. The next step on our journey of awakening is to recognize something else that we're normally too unconscious to notice . . . and that is our essential identity as the "I" of awareness.

CHAPTER 4

THE "I" OF AWARENESS

I love the creative buzz of being in the recording studio late at night. Just me and the engineer, with rows of synths to play, knobs to twiddle, and banks of lights twinkling in the semilit room. It's like being in a psychedelic spaceship, waiting for the muse to magically beam down and inspire me to make music.

I'm in my early 30s now, but I've been a musician, composer, and producer since my teens—creating everything from inspirational pop to television themes, scores for contemporary dance, and softcore house music. I'm fascinated by the way sound can change my state of consciousness. The impact of philosophy lasts longer, but the magic of music is so much more immediate.

One of my more obscure "claims to fame" is that in my 20s, I co-founded the first workers' cooperative recording studio. Actually, it was a front for an occult community . . . but that's another story. In the last few years, I've been running a multimedia collective called "World Without Walls" that has put on spectacular shamanic rave shows with a huge cast of musicians, fire jugglers, dancers, live video operators, giant puppets . . . the works.

Recently I've become fascinated with combining sound and the spoken word. I've just finished a philosophical "soundscape" featuring the voice of "hands-on pharmacologist" Terence McKenna talking about his outlandish experiences of altered states on DMT . . . the stuff they snort out of bamboo blowpipes in the Amazon jungle.

I've also done a consciousness-raising dance track featuring Ram Dass. He's one of my heroes because I love his authenticity and humor. As Richard Alpert, he was a professor at Harvard, but then he was thrown out (along with Timothy Leary) for experimenting with LSD. He went on to follow the Indian guru Neem Karoli Baba, who gave him the name "Ram Dass," which means "servant of God."

Tonight I am experimenting with combining poetry and music. I'm a devotee of Walt Whitman because I adore the way he rants incessantly about the wonders of the world until he forces me to surrender into unconditional appreciation. So I'm experimenting with reading one of his poems against a seductive beat, to see if the music enhances the effect.

I've chosen a poem called "Miracles," which I love because it is an ecstatic eulogy to the magic of everyday life. As I read to the music, I can feel the intensity building steadily, and I start to enter the mystery. This is working well. If it can take listeners to the place it's taking me as a performer, that will be great.

But then right near the end, I fluff a line. Whitman is wildly extolling the beauty of the ocean, and I've just said the word "sea" instead of "fishes." I stop and signal to the engineer that we need to start again. And while he's fussing with technical stuff, I think about what I have just said . . . "The sea that swims." It actually captures something about the paradox of oneness.

This starts me thinking about an amazing book on waking up to oneness that I've been studying for years titled *I Am That.* It's a collection of discussions with the Indian teacher Sri Nisargadatta Maharaj. His name's a bit of a mouthful, but it roughly translates to "Mr. Natural." He sold cheap cigarettes in the back streets of Mumbai. And as someone with an on/off addiction to tobacco, that makes me feel like a kindred spirit.

Mr. Natural was an audacious explorer of the mystery and an extremely articulate Advaitic philosopher. For me he's the antidote to all of those softly spoken, soporific spiritual teachers sitting next to bunches of flowers. In contrast to their bland predictability and calculated stillness, he is animated and full of personality.

I've got a wonderful video of him passionately answering difficult questions, raising his voice and stabbing the air incisively with his hands, speaking a language I don't understand. But the amusing thing is that a translation is being read over the top in pious, monotone English . . . the complete opposite of Nisargadatta's in-your-face style. This is a case study of the problem with "spirituality." The fiery eccentricity of an authentic voice is watered down into safe, sanctimonious platitudes. Revolutionary jazz turns into complacent easy listening.

The engineer is taking a long time getting ready for the next take, so I find myself going over in my mind a particularly powerful passage from Mr. Natural's book, which I've read so many times that I know it by heart:

> "You have squeezed yourself into the span of a lifetime and the volume of a body and thus created the innumerable conflicts of life and death. Have your being outside this body of birth and death, and all your problems will be solved. They exist because you believe yourself born to die. Undeceive yourself and be free. You are not a person."

The last line now jumps out at me like an electric shock. What could it possibly mean? The backing track is on a loop, repeating over and over, so I start saying "I am not a person" like a mantra to the rhythm of the music.

I AM NOT A PERSON.

This goes well with the beat.

I AM NOT A PERSON.

Could that be true?

I AM NOT A PERSON.

Oh my God, it *is* true, because I'm not really saying this, it's just happening by itself.

I AM NOT A PERSON.

I'm conscious of an unfolding flow of experience.

I AM NOT A PERSON.

So what am "I"?

I AM NOT A PERSON.

I'm a mysterious presence.

I AM NOT A PERSON.

I'm awareness witnessing this moment.

I AM NOT A PERSON.

I'm not "Tim" . . . I'm watching "Tim."

I AM NOT A PERSON.

This is very peculiar.

I AM NOT A PERSON.

Now Tim is laughing.

I AM NOT A PERSON.

He's beginning to become hysterical.

I AM NOT A PERSON.

He's collapsing on the ground in convulsions of . . . laughter or distress . . . it's impossible to tell.

I AM NOT A PERSON.

He can hardly say it now because he's breathing so quickly and deeply.

I AM NOT A PERSON.

He's starting to cry because he's disoriented and confused.

I AM NOT A PERSON.

Now he's calming down and weeping with relief.

I AM NOT A PERSON.

His breath is slowing . . . and there's a big, spacious emptiness.

I AM NOT A PERSON.

Stillness . . . wonder . . . oneness . . . love.

Then the engineer turns off the backing track and, looking a little worried, asks, "Are you okay, Tim?" Suddenly I'm a person again, lying in a crumpled heap on the floor, grinning. And the engineer tells me, "I've been recording all that, you know." So I reply, "In which case it's probably the first mystical experience ever captured live on tape."

Being Conscious of Being Conscious

The dawn is breaking, and I'm meditating peacefully in my own personal church. At least that's how I see it, since no one seems to come here but me. It's a small building with exquisite William Morris designs etched into the plaster, nestled into the quiet countryside. And unlike most English churches these days, it's left unlocked, so I can slip in whenever I like, day or night.

Recently I've become part of an experimental community of awakening, living in a huge country mansion. This place is so amazing. From my bedroom window, I can look down the long drive and see Glastonbury Tor rising up mysteriously from the Somerset levels. And from the room I'm renting for my recording studio, I can see "my" church, just beyond the lake in the garden.

Since my "I am not a person" experience the other night, I've found myself going further into the deep awake state. I'd often read in mystical literature that I'm not really the person I appear to be, because my essential identity is the impersonal "I." But that night in the studio, I actually *experienced* the truth of this. And that has changed everything.

Like many of my breakthrough deep awake experiences, this revelation happened spontaneously of itself. But now I find that I can return to this state again by letting go of the idea that I am Tim and identifying instead with the "I" of awareness, which is conscious of Tim and all that he experiences.

Nisargadatta recommends this technique, which is taught by many spiritual traditions. Sometimes it's called "witnessing" or "mindfulness." I see it as simply being conscious that I'm conscious. For me, this practice involves first disengaging my attention from the story of Tim and entering the mystery of the moment. Then I become conscious of my essential nature as the "I" of awareness, which is witnessing an unfolding flow of experiences.

Right now I'm sitting alone in my church, practicing "being conscious of being conscious" . . .

I'm conscious that I'm witnessing...
I'm aware that I'm witnessing...
The "I" of Awareness

awareness/consciousness witnesses

I'm witnessing my body breathing in and out.

I'm witnessing my thoughts coming and going.

I'm witnessing the sound of the birds singing in the church-yard.

I'm witnessing the silence reverberating around this beautiful old building.

I'm witnessing the light cast by the stained-glass windows, dancing in kaleidoscopic patterns on the stone floor.

I am conscious that my essential nature is awareness, witness-ing everything I'm experiencing right now.

I am conscious of being a still presence, witnessing a flow of ever-changing appearances.

I am conscious of how amazing it is that I'm experiencing anything at all.

I am conscious that I feel in love with the miracle of life.

I am conscious of the bliss of just *being*.

Until eventually I start witnessing that my bum has gone numb sitting on the hard wooden pew . . . and I decide it's time to move.

The Presence of Awareness

Transcending the personal self and becoming conscious of our deeper identity is the next step on our journey of awakening. So I want to share with you a couple of great quotes from two different spiritual traditions that point us to our essential nature. The first is from a wonderful Hindu text called *The Chandogya Upanishad,* in which the sage Uddalaka Aruni presents an interesting riddle:

"What is it that can't be seen,
but which makes seeing possible?
What is it that can't be heard,
but which makes hearing possible?
What is it that can't be known,
but which makes knowledge possible?
What is it that can't be imagined,
but which makes imagination possible?"

The second is a quote is from the Gnostic *Gospel of Thomas,* in which Jesus makes a startling promise, reminiscent of Uddalaka Aruni's riddle:

"I will reveal to you
what can't be seen,
what can't be heard,
what can't be touched,
what can't be imagined."

What is it we can't see, hear, touch, or imagine? I want to suggest that the answer is "awareness." Awareness can't be seen but makes seeing possible. Awareness can't be heard but makes hearing possible. Awareness can't be imagined but makes imagining possible. Awareness is the permanent background to our ever-changing experiences. It is a mysterious presence that is witnessing this flow of colors, shapes, sounds, and thoughts we call "life."

Awareness is our essential *being.* The Hindus call it the *atman,* which means "self." Christians call it *spirit,* which means "essence." Buddhists call it the *Buddha-nature,* which means "knower-nature." When I understand what these exotic terms really refer to, I can see that self-knowledge is simpler than I had imagined. Knowing my essential self is knowing the knower. It is recognizing my deeper identity as awareness.

what is the knower like?
I'm that —

46

But how do we become conscious of our essential nature? Awareness isn't something we can see, hear, touch, or imagine. We can't know our deeper identity objectively, since awareness isn't an object in our experience. But we can subjectively know ourselves to be the experiencer. And we can do this by simply becoming conscious of being conscious. This is the wake-up technique known as "witnessing."

Sometimes when I hear people talking about witnessing, it can *not* sound like a disconnected state in which they become aloof observ- *aloof* ers of life. But this is not what I experience. When I practice "being conscious of being conscious," I don't just watch my experience, I find myself *appreciating* my experience. Nisargadatta calls this *turiya*, which can be translated as "detached but affectionate awareness."

the story of Jane

Let's practice appreciative witnessing right now . . .

You are conscious that you're experiencing something . . . so pay attention to the experiencer. *the one who experiences - the one in the background exp'ins*

Focus on your essential *being* that you call "I," which is the constant background to all you experience.
- *aware*
- *witnessing*

Consciously *be* the presence of awareness, witnessing the mystery of this moment.
- *the watcher*
- *non-judgmental*

This doesn't mean cutting yourself off from your experience as an aloof observer; your experience is not separate from what you are any more than a dream is separate from the dreamer. *I set it up.*

Consciously *be* the presence of awareness and embrace your experience of this moment with love and acceptance.

Consciously *be* the presence of awareness, witnessing and appreciating the feeling of your breath rising and falling.

Consciously *be* the presence of awareness, witnessing and appreciating what you are seeing. *non judgmentally unafraid (curious? interested?) not invested in the story (except for love?)*

(• wise, compassionate, loving)

Consciously *be* the presence of awareness, witnessing and appreciating what you are hearing.

Consciously *be* the presence of awareness, witnessing and appreciating your thoughts.

Consciously *be* the "I" of awareness, witnessing and appreciating the person you appear to be.

Take some time to try this for yourself, and then ask what you can say about your essential nature as awareness. You can't see it or hear it or touch it. It has no qualities or characteristics, because it isn't something within your experience. Your essential nature is absolutely mysterious.

If you step out of your story and enter deeply into the mystery of the moment, you'll begin to recognize your essential nature, since your deepest being *is* the mystery. If you practice witnessing, you'll become conscious of being the "I" of awareness, which isn't a part of your experience because it's the presence within which experiences are arising. If you take your attention away from the dream, you will become conscious of being the dreamer who isn't in the dream.

I'm watching my own creation unfolding w/in
(the creator)   presence

Big Mind   *I'm a spectator!*

Mystics of all traditions claim that if we become conscious of our essential nature, we will realize that in reality, there is only one of us. There is one Self experiencing itself to be many individual selves. There is one Big Mind, as the Zen masters say, within which the dream of life is arising.

As a philosopher, I'm a big fan of both spirituality and science. When I first began to see life as like a dream arising within one universal awareness, I felt as if I were being forced to reject the scientific paradigm. But since then, I've become acquainted with the ideas of some of the greatest physicists who have shaped our modern understanding of the universe. And what I have found has astonished me.

Often science and spirituality are seen as irreconcilably different approaches to understanding life, but they are actually complementary ways of exploring the mystery of existence. Science adopts an objective perspective on reality and is concerned with understanding the world of appearances. Spirituality adopts a subjective perspective on reality and is concerned with exploring states of consciousness.

What fascinates me is that the great physicists' objective investigations of the world have ultimately led them to very similar conclusions to the ones I have reached through my subjective investigation of consciousness. In the popular mind, the scientific worldview is often presumed to be materialistic and contrary to esoteric mystical claims, such as life being a dream in one great mind. But nothing could be further from the truth. Take a look at this remarkable statement:

> "The universe begins to look more like a great thought than like a great machine."

This is not an outrageous flight of fancy from some flaky New Ager. It's the considered conclusion of Sir James Jeans, who made important contributions to the dynamic theory of gases, the mathematical theory of electromagnetism, the evolution of gaseous stars, and the nature of the nebulae. And he's not alone. Check out this bold declaration:

> "The idea of a universal Mind . . . would be, I think, a fairly plausible inference from the present state of scientific theory . . ."

These are the words of Sir Arthur Eddington, who made important contributions to the theoretical physics of stellar systems and was a leading exponent of relativity. And here's another great quote:

> "As a man who has devoted his whole life to the most clear-headed science, to the study of matter, I can tell you as a result of my research into atoms this much. There is no matter as such. All matter originates and exists only by virtue of a force which brings the particles of the atom to vibration. I

must assume behind this force the existence of a conscious and intelligent mind. This mind is the matrix of all matter."

That's from a speech Max Planck, winner of the Nobel Prize for Physics, made decades ago. And this quote is from another Nobel Prize winner, Erwin Schrödinger, whose work forms the heart of quantum mechanics:

"We do not belong to this material world that science constructs for us. We are not in it; we are outside. We are only spectators. The reason why we believe that we are in it, that we belong to the picture, is that our bodies are in the picture."

It seems that for almost a century now, the pioneers of physics have been endorsing the seemingly outlandish idea that life is like a dream arising in one awareness. But this has gone largely unnoticed by mainstream society—and even scientists working in other disciplines—because it so utterly undermines our commonsense notion of who we are and what life is.

At their deepest core, physics and spirituality offer complementary insights into the nature of reality. Physics gives us an objective understanding of the "universal mind." Spirituality helps us to actually experience the "universal mind." And doing just that is the next step on our journey of awakening.

○ ○ ○

Im so identified as my body that wherever it seems to be, I think I am too. This is just a simple mistake

not perception (thats a soul exp)

CHAPTER 5

WAKING UP
TO ONENESS

This state-of-the-art hospital seems out of place in such a small Indian village. I'm waiting to hear news about my girlfriend, Tori, who is being treated by a doctor. The hospital is strangely quiet and empty, and I'm alone, apart from an American gentleman sitting opposite me. He's reading a book that keeps catching my eye. I don't want to seem rude, but I can't help staring at the cover and I don't know why. The book has magnetized my attention. Something peculiar is going on.

I am in the village of Puttaparthi, home to Sathya Sai Baba, the most famous guru in India. Isaac Tigrett, who co-founded the Hard Rock Café chain, gave him a huge amount of money to build this beautiful hospital, but hardly anyone seems to be here right now. It's all very surreal.

I've been staying at Sai Baba's ashram with my girlfriend and my retired parents, who have come along to see southern India. Sai Baba is revered as an incarnation of Vishnu . . . a living God. He produces holy ash magically from his hands . . . I've seen him do it right before my eyes. This ashram is a refuge for many thousands of his happy followers . . . and I'm *hating* it.

I'm trying not to show my discomfort because Tori is a devotee of Sai Baba, but I'm sure she can sense that this place is much too religious for me. I feel uncomfortable around all of these devotees trying to be holy. I can understand their devotion because I was an enthusiastic devotee of a super-guru myself when I was younger. It was an intense and exhilarating experience at the time, but I'm glad I escaped. And in retrospect, it burdened me with some insidious ideas that troubled me for years.

Most of our time in the ashram has been spent lining up to see Sai Baba. On a number of occasions I've been "blessed" by being allocated a front-row seat close to the man himself. I certainly enjoy his charismatic presence. But I keep thinking how much he looks like an aged Jimi Hendrix because of his hair. And that makes it hard for me to take things seriously.

Mostly he just walks around in front of his devotees and does the magic ash trick. However, I did hear him speak once on Christmas Day, which seemed an auspicious time to be in the presence of "God made flesh." He discoursed at length and was simultaneously translated into English. But he talked so quickly that the translator couldn't keep up, and soon they were both talking at the same time. Then even the Indians couldn't understand a word he was saying, so they got bored and started talking among themselves. It wasn't what I expected it would be like to listen to an enlightened Godman.

I've come to India hoping for some guidance on how to go deeper into the "I am not a person" realization I experienced a few months ago, but I don't think Sai Baba is going to be of much help. I find it frustrating that I can only watch as part of a huge crowd when what I feel I really need is a meaningful one-to-one conversation.

I love reading Nisargadatta's dialogues in the book *I Am That* because they are authentic discussions with a small group of people who ask him searching questions and argue with his answers. It's a shame that "Mr. Natural" is dead, because that questioning spirit is what attracts me.

It seems that no one doubts things or asks difficult questions in Puttaparthi. Everyone seems happy to obey the rules, no matter how crazy. When Tori got sick, for example, I was delighted to find that an

Indian doctor happened to live next door to us in the ashram. But he wouldn't tend to Tori because she was a woman and he was a man, so it wasn't allowed. How mad is that?!

When I eventually carried her into this hospital, two Indian devotees tried hard to prevent me from coming in, since I was a man entering through the women's entrance. The fact that my girlfriend could hardly stand didn't seem of any consequence. But her health was more important to me than their sexual paranoia, so I pushed my way through and found an Australian doctor who could see that she needed urgent attention.

Now I am sitting and waiting while she is being treated, and I've become obsessed with this book the American guy is reading. Why am I so attracted to it? There's nothing special about the way it looks. Eventually I get over my English reserve and ask politely,

"I'm sorry to disturb you, but what is that book?"

I am taken by surprise when he replies,

"Have you ever heard of Sri Nisargadatta Maharaj?"

I tell him I most certainly have and that I regard him as one of the greatest philosophers of the 20th century. So he explains:

"This book is written by one of his students, Ramesh Balsekar. Not many people know about him, but I think he's extraordinary. He's a retired banker who lives in Mumbai. He sees people in his flat for a few hours most mornings. You should go see him while you're in India. I'll give you his address if you want."

It's an extraordinary moment. I feel as if the universe has been listening in to my wish list and decided, on this occasion, to give me what I want. We are due to fly back to England in two days via Mumbai. If Tori is okay to travel and we leave immediately, I could just about have time to see Ramesh while I'm in India. It would be a crazy rush, but it might be doable. Hell, it's worth a try.

It seems that my time in Puttaparthi has ended up being strangely magical after all, so I don't know what to think anymore. And that feels good, because when I know I don't know, I start to wake up.

Everything Is Happening

Tori and I have left my parents at the Mumbai airport because we need to move fast, otherwise we won't get to our destination in time. They head off to find a hotel for the night while we hail a motorized rickshaw, known locally as a "Tuc-Tuc," and begin a hair-raising journey through the noisy streets. Tuc-Tuc drivers always seem to have a secret death wish, swerving and weaving around other vehicles as if they're racing in a rally. But on this occasion I'm in a hurry, so I don't mind.

When we arrive, I purchase some flowers from a street vendor, as I've been told that it's good form in India to arrive with a gift for the teacher. And then, feeling self-conscious with this bouquet in my hand, I ring the bell for the address scrawled on the crumpled piece of paper I'm clutching. We're later than I'd hoped, but we're here.

We're ushered into a modest flat by a friendly-looking American. Inside are seated a few Westerners, mostly Germans; along with a distinguished-looking, white-haired Indian gentleman in a rocking chair. I feel excited and alert, as if something significant is about to happen.

Ramesh Balsekar has an unpretentious air of calm authority. He's very different from Nisargadatta, and that's a good sign. I like the idea of this sophisticated, retired president of the Bank of India choosing to become the student of someone who sells cheap cigarettes in the slums.

As we come in, Ramesh welcomes us politely and, abandoning the conversation he was having before we arrived, makes it clear that he now intends to talk with me. It all starts in a casual way, with him asking me what I do for a living. I explain that I've recently become an author. He seems mildly intrigued and inquires how that came about. I say, "It just happened," and he smiles broadly, as if this reply tells him something he needs to know.

I go on to explain that my first book has just been published. It's a new version of the Tao Te Ching, an ancient Chinese work by a legendary master named Lao-tzu, which I've been studying since my teens. I'd wanted to read this enigmatic text over a soundscape, as part of my experiments with music and the spoken word, but I hadn't been able to find a translation that felt right, so I'd done my own interpretation. An author friend suggested that I send the manuscript to his literary agent to explore the possibility of getting it published. By some strange coincidence, my book arrived on the agent's desk at the same time as a letter from a publisher saying that they were looking for a new version of the Tao Te Ching.

Ramesh ignores the others in the room and listens attentively. Then he asks me very directly, "So, Tim, what can I do for you?" The atmosphere in the room is electric. Intuitively, I'm sure that this is my opportunity for an in-depth exchange with a philosopher who really knows what he's talking about. So I relate my recent "I am not a person" experience and await his comments.

For the next hour, Ramesh and I engage in an intense dialogue that I know will change my life. I am with a man who has clearly seen through the illusion of separateness. He paints a vision of the world in which everything is occurring as an unfolding oneness. There really is no "Tim" who is a separate individual with his own free will. The person I appear to be is a part of nature. Ramesh is talking and Tim is listening in the same natural way that the sun is shining and the world is turning. There is no little man inside my head who is choosing to say this or do that. There is no "doer."

Ramesh is guiding me into a profound understanding of the perennial teachings of "no self." But time and again, in his lilting Indian accent he reminds me, "Make no mistake about it, these are only concepts." He wants to make sure we don't get stuck in a futile intellectual argument. He wants me to see beyond the ideas and enter into the mystery. . . . Although, thinking about it, I'm not sure he actually *wants* anything. He's seems to just be enjoying the play.

Ramesh's words "There is no doer" are reverberating in my mind, just as Nisargadatta's "You are not a person" had done previously. I've always presumed that Tim was a volitional agent who makes choices,

I remember the *leg* of Mary, Sed & relieved at the same time that the one I thought of as *fen* seller who ent of a job in this capacity. Steven became funny + sad too.

HOW LONG IS NOW?

this loss of identity

no doer

but now I see things differently. As I pay attention to the moment, I'm conscious that my thoughts are just arising. I'm not doing the think-ing. Thinking is happening. And as all of my volitional actions arise from my thoughts, that means that they are just happening as well.

In a rush of realization, I get what Ramesh is saying to me. The recognition of "no doer" is waking me up to oneness. Except that there is no "Tim" to wake up. The waking up is happening. I feel quiet elation, unconditional acceptance, and a profound sense of relief. I'm free from judgment, because there is no one to blame. I'm free from guilt, because there is no one to reproach. I'm no longer a seeker on a spiritual quest, because there's no one to be lost or enlightened. And that realization *is* enlightenment . . . but it's not happening to anyone . . . and that's very funny.

When the time comes to go, I feel more grateful than I can pos-sibly say. Then Ramesh takes me into an adjoining room and gives me a copy of the book that the American was reading in Puttaparthi. It's a translation of a Sanskrit text called *The Ashtavakra Gita,* which Ramesh has titled *A Duet of One.* That's a great title because it perfectly captures the paradox of our conversation together.

As I leave, people come up excitedly to tell me that this was one of the best dialogues they'd ever heard. And they assure me Ramesh had been hinting that I was definitely going to "get the understand-ing." But that seems a funny idea, as there is no "me" to get anything. Everything will naturally unfold as it must. There's no Tim to do any-thing about it.

Tori has enjoyed meeting Ramesh, but for me it's been a semi-nal experience. I can't believe that my understanding has been trans-formed so radically in just one hour. Ramesh has helped me really penetrate the simple essence of the philosophy of Advaita or "not two." I smile at the thought that, having written a version of the Tao Te Ching, I've just met a living Lao-tzu. A man who knows that all is one flow of life . . . the Tao . . . the way of things.

As Tori and I walk out into the noisy city, I feel as if I'm floating rather than walking because my legs seem to be moving by them-selves. I need to sit quietly and digest what has just happened, so I look around for somewhere to escape the noise and the burning Indian sun. Across the busy road I see a large bookstore, and I suggest that we go in. As we enter, I feel the cool breeze of the air-conditioning. Then something catches my eye, and I stop still in amazement.

My new version of the Tao Te Ching is the first book I've had published, and I've secretly been looking forward to coming across it for sale in a bookstore. This has never happened because it's only one minor publication among thousands of books printed every week. But now, all this way from home, after having just met an embodiment of Taoist wisdom, there in front of me, prominently displayed at the entrance to the store . . . is my book.

no Tim, no doer
no Jane, no doer – how sad
how happy

The Play of Forms

It is many years now since I met Ramesh, and I still find that when I see there's "no doer," I wake up to oneness. In the oneness of things, there are no separate individuals to do this or that. Everything is one flow of forms. Take a look for yourself right now:

Sink into the mystery of the moment and become conscious of being conscious.

Be awareness . . . witnessing a flow of colors, shapes, sounds, and thoughts.

I am no-thing : formless

Let go of the idea of yourself as a "doer" of anything, and instead passively witness everything happening.

Recognize that your experience is one evolving event in which everything is unfolding as it must. *w/o "Jane" the ego & personality*

Your eyes are reading these words as a natural part of the one flow of appearances.

Your thoughts and reactions are arising as a natural part of the one flow of appearances.

Your separate identity as a person is an integral part of the impersonal play of forms.

From this perspective there is no "you" choosing to do this or that. You are awareness passively witnessing the world.

All is one and you are that oneness.

No One Is Enlightened

I will always be grateful to Ramesh for showing me that the paradoxical secret of enlightenment is to recognize that there is no "Tim" to be enlightened, since all is one. This was a momentous realization, which transformed my understanding of the journey of awakening. Previously I had felt that there was something I had to do in order to wake up to oneness. Ironically, it turned out that the opposite was true. I needed to see that there was "no doer."

I had often had powerful intimations of oneness when I entered the deep awake state—but now I found myself immersed in oneness, and the separate individual known as "Tim" seemed less and less important. I felt that my journey of awakening was over because I'd seen that there was no one to make the journey. I soon discovered that I was wrong about this and that there was much farther to go. But before I explore all of that, I want to tell you about Ramesh's last words to me, because they make me laugh.

That's Not Going to Happen

It is the morning after my first meeting with Ramesh and we've just had time to squeeze in another brief conversation, which has grounded my understanding from yesterday. Now I'm saying thank you and good-bye, as we're flying to England in a few hours. As we leave, I offer Ramesh a copy of my Tao Te Ching, which I'd come across so synchronistically in the bookstore. He declines, saying that he already has too many books, so I give it to the friendly American, who seems very pleased. Then I take the opportunity to ask Ramesh one last question:

"What should I do now?"

As I speak, I realize that this is a silly question. Ramesh has just spent the last two hours telling me that there's nothing to do because everything is just happening. He answers in an offhand way,

"Don't worry about it. Go home. Get on with your life. Get married and have children."

I smile politely while I think to myself,

That's not going to happen.

CHAPTER 6

Wonderful sort of earth philosophy

I'm making sense of the paradox?
• Cool detachment / personal warmth
• Compassion / affection

• impersonal oneness / personal world

FAMILY LIFE

It is Good Friday. The candles are twinkling, and Allegri's "Miserere" is playing softly. I'm holding my wife, Debbie, to support her body in the birthing pool. She is serenely exhausted and radiantly feminine. The baby is tenderly resting on Debbie's breasts, and her tiny nose is almost touching my own. I can feel her gentle breath against my cheek. In the presence of such innocence, I am humbled by awe. Then her eyes open for the first time and look straight into mine.

Her pupils are black passageways to endless emptiness, and I dive in. I'm swimming in an ocean of mystery. This is the moment of our meeting; and I am instantly, utterly, unconditionally in love. I would die for my daughter without hesitation. I will devote my life to her until my last breath. I have traveled the world in search of meaning and wonders, yet here in the familiarity of my own front room is a greater miracle than I had ever dreamed possible.

A few days ago I had been driving in the car when the song "She's the One" by Robbie Williams had come on the radio, and I suddenly began to weep uncontrollably. I knew that I was soon to meet the most important woman in my life, and now here she is. More perfect than I could have imagined. So beautiful that tears are once more flooding into my eyes.

I am in my early 40s and have adored being a dad ever since I met Debbie and adopted her young son, Beau, three years ago. I fell instantly in love with both of them, as I have now with this angel before me. Previously I'd never considered becoming a father. Family life was not for me because I was too busy playing at the edge. Now I am so grateful that my life hasn't worked out as I'd planned.

The midwife passes the baby to Beau, who is now five, and he cradles his sister in his safe young arms. I love them so much it hurts. He had told us confidently that the baby would be a girl born at Easter, but we hadn't believed him because she was due weeks before. Yet Beau was right. And it feels a significant coincidence that I'm writing a book about Sophia, the Christian Goddess of Wisdom in Gnostic mythology, because here I am face-to-face with the Goddess incarnate. We'll call her "Sophia" because that's already her name. This is a very good Friday indeed. The best day of my life.

The World of Poo

It's the middle of the night, and I'm stumbling from our bedroom to the bathroom with a very wet baby in one hand and a fresh diaper in the other. The baby is crying, and the pitch is so piercing that it seems perfectly designed to make her impossible to ignore. How can such a loud sound come from such a small mouth? I don't know how Debbie manages to filter it out and stay asleep. But I'm glad she does, or at least pretends to, because she's even more exhausted than I am and desperately needs to rest.

I arrive semiconsciously in the bathroom and place the baby on the changing mat to remove her diaper. It's oozing with sickly, sweet-smelling poo. But any squeamishness about bodily functions soon disappeared once I began this journey to the land of urine, feces, and vomit. I clean her, put on the new diaper, and the crying stops. Then I stagger back to the bedroom and place her in her crib.

She is quiet now, and I sit gazing at her minute features. Being a dad is demanding, but I do all of this without hesitation. I would do anything for this bundle of tears and smiles. I'm her willing servant. I feel as if I'm in the presence of a little Buddha who is teaching me the true meaning of love.

My tired thoughts begin to explore the irony of my new life. I can't meditate for days as I used to when I had plenty of time on my hands. I'm too busy with domestic life and "bringing home the bacon" . . . or in my case, the vegetarian substitute. Yet I feel more alive than ever, although often there's not much space for feeling spacious. This is not what I expected.

When I was younger, I had the idea that if I wanted to be a "first class" spiritual seeker, I needed to become some sort of monk and dedicate myself wholeheartedly to the quest for enlightenment. An ordinary life in the world as a "householder" was for "second class" seekers who weren't up to taking on the real challenge. Now I feel the opposite is true.

I wanted to be a monk so that I could immerse myself in divine love. Now I'm a parent and feeling so much natural affection that my heart is overflowing. I wanted to sacrifice my life at the altar of selfless service. Now I find myself changing diapers in the middle of the night, without any thought for myself and how fatigued I feel, willingly giving myself away to this other being whom I care for. And there's nothing spiritual about it. It's all perfectly natural.

Cool Detachment and Human Warmth

Beau and I have been play-fighting too boisterously and have just knocked over a bookcase, creating chaos in the house. Debbie has rescued Beau from the trauma with comfort and kisses, leaving me sitting in a pile of books. I pick one up to begin the process of putting them back in their place. It's a title on Zen that I've had for years, and I can't resist flicking through the pages.

It opens on a teaching story I know well, because I used to find it inspiring. But as I think about it now, I find it somewhat disturbing . . .

"There once was a young girl who fell pregnant by a boy. In her panic to protect him, she claimed that the father was a much-revered Buddhist monk who lived as a hermit on the mountain by their village. The villagers were outraged, and when the baby was born, they took it up the mountain to confront the monk. They said, 'This is your child, so you can support it, not us.' And with tranquil acceptance, he took the child and simply said, 'So be it.'"

Thus far the story still works for me. I'd like to be this serene sage, lovingly allowing life to be as it is. But there's more. . . .

"Many years later, the girl felt such shame that she confessed her lie. The villagers were mortified at what they had done. So they went back to the monk, asked his forgiveness, and told him that they would take the child and bring him up themselves. And with sublime detachment, the monk replied, 'So be it.'"

When I read this teaching story in my youth, I longed to achieve such superhuman detachment. But now I have an adopted son myself, and if anyone comes knocking on my door to take him away from me, I'm not going to say, "So be it." I'm going to tell them, "No f*cking way!"

I can't help feeling there is something missing from a philosophy that values cool detachment more than the warmth of personal attachment. I place the book on Zen back on the shelf. It's been important to me in the past, but the ideas now seem alien, from another time and culture. Being a dad is changing me, for it's making me realize how much I love this dream of separateness.

Looking at the books spread around me, I feel forced to face the fact that there is something wrong with the perennial philosophy of oneness I've been studying all these years. At its core there is an implicit, and sometimes explicit, rejection of the world and the personal life. Here's a volume about the Buddha, who abandoned his family to become a celibate monk. Here's one about Jesus, who told his disciples to leave their families and follow him. Well, I'm sorry, guys, but I'm not up for that. I don't think it's necessary, and I don't feel it's right.

Beau is back and helping me return the books to the shelf. The one in my hands is called *Non-Dual Enlightenment*. The spiritual traditions often say that we must want enlightenment more than we want anything else. But I don't want to be enlightened more than I want to care for my children. If I have to choose between my personal life and impersonal oneness, then I choose being Tim with his family and everyday worries. But I don't want to make this choice—I want to *both* wake up to oneness *and* passionately engage with my personal life as a separate individual.

In my hand now is *A Duet of One* by Ramesh Balsekar, which I place on the shelf next to *I Am That* by Sri Nisargadatta Maharaj. And this makes me feel confused about my "choice." If everything is just happening, then choice is illusory. I have seen this to be true in my own direct experience. Yet I also experience the reality of personal choice in every moment. I need a new philosophy that can help me reconcile these two different realities. The traditional philosophy of awakening has taught me how to see through the illusion of separateness to the primal oneness. But now I want to articulate a philosophy that also reflects my love of the life-dream.

Feminine Wisdom

My wife and I are enjoying the rare treat of going out for a meal together because my mum is babysitting the kids. She's a wonderful grandma and they love her to bits. Debbie is taking a long time deciding what to order, as she usually does, but I'm enjoying the opportunity to feast my eyes on her beautiful features. Since she introduced me to family life, my world has become so much richer, and I'm so grateful.

What I love about Debbie is that she's different from me. She doesn't think about everything like I do, but she can be very insightful. She isn't overtly spiritual; she's just full of love. My mother is the same. And I'm in awe of their natural feminine wisdom.

As I get older, I'm seeing things with new eyes, which gives me a new perspective on my past. One of the things I liked about Ramesh was that he was a family man, not a celibate swami in orange robes. But looking back, I feel that something is missing from his philosophy, or at least my understanding of it. The vision of life as an impersonal oneness is wonderfully liberating, but it can seem so cold that it makes me shiver.

I remember a woman in Mumbai whose husband had died, so she'd come to India to put his ashes in the Ganges. She was clearly grieving and asked Ramesh what she should do. He told her to forget it and see through the illusion of the separate self. This made me uncomfortable, and I was relieved when the kind American went up to comfort her afterward. I wonder how I would have felt had it been my loved one's ashes in that urn?

And then there was a girl who asked, "What about love?" Ramesh gave the offhand reply, "Love is the opposite of hate," and changed the subject. But for me, love is much more than that. Since my deep awake experience as a boy, love has always been at the heart of my life. When I'm deep awake, I'm overwhelmed by love. The importance of love is the one thing I've always been sure of.

When I came back from my meeting with Ramesh, I was so enthusiastic about what he'd shown me that I told all of my friends, including Theo Simon and Shannon Smy from the protest folk band Seize The Day. Theo and Shannon were going to India, so they visited Ramesh in Mumbai. Just like when Tori and I talked with Ramesh, Theo really got the vision of the impersonal oneness, but Shannon didn't. At the time I thought that the girls had missed out. But it seems to me now that these women were picking up on something we men didn't notice.

Here's one way of seeing the situation: masculine wisdom is about communing with the impersonal oneness, but feminine wisdom is about loving the personal world. When I think about my family, I know that I want both. I want to wake up to oneness *and* fully engage with the intimate dramas of my personal life. This is what my own baby Goddess has taught me.

Universal Compassion and Personal Affection

I've taken my thoughts out for a walk into the quiet of the night. Something is wrong, and that feels right. I am on fire with cleansing confusion. I welcome this bewilderment because it is propelling me to see more about my paradoxical life. I need to find a philosophy of oneness that's big enough to embrace my love of separateness.

The hour is late, and my way is lit by lamplight so bright that it obscures the stars. I find myself fascinated by the rows of endless houses. The town is deserted because everyone has retreated into a small, homey world enclosed by four walls. And I'm imagining what lies behind the curtains that cover the windows.

Different people, different lives, all with their own personal loves and particular problems. Each house unique, and yet each house the same . . . full of longing and relief, conflict and forgiveness, betrayal and devotion, anxiety and heroism, numbness and passion, terror and TV. I adore the muddled richness of this poignant dream.

I love these strangers in their own private boxes, even though I'll probably never meet them. I've sought to nurture this unconditional compassion throughout my life, but now it's clear that I also want personal affection. I need to love and be loved by this particular woman because she is *my* wife and by these particular children because they are *my* kids.

The traditional philosophy of oneness has a great deal to say about universal love. But there doesn't seem to be much room for personal love. And that troubles me. . . . Then I stop in my tracks in front of a piece of graffiti sprayed on the churchyard wall. It makes me smile because it captures my realization that generalized compassion alone just isn't enough:

> "JESUS LOVES YOU
> but then he loves everyone."

○ ○ ○

CHAPTER 7

LUCID LIVING

The view is beautiful. I'm in Northern Ireland, in a town called Newcastle, where "the Mountains of Mourne sweep down to the sea" as the old song puts it. I'm in my early 40s and I'm gazing out at the turbulent ocean from the balcony of a sparkling-new flat, where I am staying for a couple of weeks to work on a book I want to write.

The flat has been lent to me by an amazing gentleman named Des Rice, who has also bought me a brand-new Mac laptop to work on. Another dear friend, Sean Reynolds, has become my "patron," and that's given me a year without financial worries to really develop my ideas. My life as a philosopher would be impossible without such generous support.

Over the last decade I've written many books on spiritual philosophy, showing that all of the mystical traditions of the world are fundamentally about waking up to oneness. In recent years, I've become best known for my popular academic books on Christian Gnosticism, written with my old friend Peter Gandy.

It's been a privilege to do this work with him, since I feel that it's immensely important to completely revise the traditional understanding of Christianity. But my real passion is for the mystery of the moment . . . not the past. And that's why I'm here in Northern Ireland working on a book of philosophy that is rooted in an experiential examination of the now.

I want to find a way to take people to the state I am experiencing myself, in which I'm *both* conscious that all is one *and* in love with the story of separateness. But I'm finding this very hard to do because it's easy for my ideas to come across as convoluted and abstract, even though they really are very simple and totally experiential.

While working on my last book, *Jesus and the Lost Goddess,* I began to articulate a philosophy about both waking up to oneness and celebrating separateness, based on my interpretation of ancient Gnosticism. I'm very proud of this book because it breaks new ground in so many ways. But there's no denying that parts of it can be difficult to read, since it draws upon archaic concepts from the distant past. And this has made me want to write a book that explores this philosophy in a contemporary way . . . free from all of that outdated jargon.

The Ocean of Oneness

As I sit here on the balcony watching the ocean, I'm reminded of a verse from Ramesh's translation of *The Ashtavakra Gita:*

"How remarkable! In Me, the limitless ocean, the waves of individual selves arise according to their inherent nature, meet and play with one another for a while and then disappear."

That's a powerful image, and I know exactly what it means. The ground of being is like an ocean of unconscious awareness, arising as individual waves of consciousness. The conscious waves seem separate, but the oceanic depths are one. In the normal waking state, I'm conscious of being the wave; but in the deep awake state, I'm also conscious of being the unfathomable ocean.

I am a conscious wave, rising and falling from the unconscious depths each day when I wake and sleep. While I'm awake, I believe that I'm choosing my direction as I make my journey of life before I crash upon the shoreline of death. But actually everything I do is no more than an impersonal eddy in the great sea of being.

I love these sorts of analogies because they help me picture the ineffable. But most analogies only work up to a point, and often carry unwanted implications. This metaphor, for example, is perfect for conveying our essential oneness. Yet it makes my individual nature seem pretty irrelevant, and that doesn't feel right to me. Surely "Tim" is more than merely temporary surf on the churning deep.

The ocean metaphor is extremely picturesque, but it's not very experiential. I find it hard to actually see myself as a wave when I examine my real experience. I want to find an analogy that can help me understand the relationship between oneness and separateness in an experiential way, without devaluing separateness.

When I met Ramesh, the Advaitic philosophy of oneness was not being widely explored in Western spiritual circles, but things are changing. Now there are many Western Neo-Advaitic teachers who have popularized these ideas, many of whom are very good. The irony for me, however, is that as Advaitic philosophy has become more widely embraced, I have found myself feeling that it's missing something important, especially when it paints our personal lives as some meaningless fantasy to be transcended.

I understand the temptation to reject separateness in order to wake up to oneness. Separateness is sticky. I find it easy to get caught up in the dramas of life and forget that it's possible to wake up, so sometimes I want to push separateness away to escape its limiting clutches. But all of this changes when I become deep awake, because for me this is an experience of all-embracing big love. Suddenly, I find that what was a prison becomes a playground. I love the "illusion" of life. I don't want out; I want to go farther in. I want to really appreciate the wonders of Tim's individual existence.

Conscious Dreaming

I'm sitting in the flat at the dining table that has become my temporary desk, flicking through the pile of papers in front of me. I've written about 20,000 words for this book, but I'm not happy with it.

I want to write a much smaller book that captures the very essence of the philosophy I've been developing, like the ones that have had a big impact on me, such as the Tao Te Ching. I want my new book to be concise, clear, and accessible, so I need a simple way of conveying my ideas.

And that's when my attention is drawn to one particular paragraph in my manuscript, and I feel a rush of excitement. The metaphor I need has been staring me in the face all along. I'd written about it in passing, but I hadn't realized what I'd done. I take this page and throw the rest of the manuscript into the trash. I've just found what I'm looking for, so all of my previous work has now been reduced to wastepaper. But I'm not fed up; I'm thrilled.

In the paragraph I've kept from my redundant manuscript, I compare waking up to "lucid dreaming." All of a sudden, this seems the perfect analogy to make the foundation of my philosophy. When I'm in the deep awake state, I experience what could be called "lucid living."

Most of the time when I dream, I'm engrossed in my dream dramas, but occasionally I realize I'm dreaming and know that I'm Tim imagining my dreamworld. This is lucid dreaming. Likewise, in the waking state I'm usually engrossed in my waking dramas, but sometimes I'm also conscious of the deep awake state of oneness. I know that life is not what it seems—I can see that it's like a collective dream. I find myself living lucidly.

The beauty of this analogy is that it allows me to clearly see that I have two poles to my identity . . .

In a dream, I appear to be my dream persona, but really I'm the dreamer.

In the waking state, it's the same: I appear to be Tim, but my deeper identity is awareness, within which the dream of life is arising.

When I dream lucidly, although I'm experiencing the dream from the perspective of my dream persona, I know that I'm really the dreamer, so I'm one with everything and everyone in the dream.

when I live lucidly I know I'm exp'ng the world from my dine persona, yet I also know I'm prl mal awareness exp'ing myself as one w/all

Lucid Living

In the same way, when I live lucidly, I know that although I'm experiencing the waking world from the perspective of my waking persona, I'm the primal awareness that is one with everything and everyone.

When I dream lucidly, I know that I am *both* a separate individual in the dreamworld *and* that I'm one with everything in the dream.

When I live lucidly, I know that I am *both* a separate individual in the waking world *and* that I am one with everything in the life-dream. *+ the primal awareness,*

The analogy of lucid living really works for me because it fits with my actual experience of being deep awake. And it helps me picture how we can both wake up to oneness and engage with our personal lives as separate individuals.

When I dream lucidly, the dream continues. Indeed, I don't want the dream to end because I'm enjoying it. It's similar when I'm deep awake and living lucidly. I see the dreamlike nature of life, but the life-dream doesn't stop. And I don't want it to stop, because when I'm deep awake, I truly appreciate the magic of existence.

When I live lucidly, I find myself in the paradoxical predicament of being in the life-dream but not in the life-dream at the same time. What happens in the life-dream matters *and* doesn't matter. I'm *this is a dance of paradox* attached *and* unattached. I'm neither lost in the drama nor detached and uncaring. I'm engaged with my life but also free and spacious.

When I read mystical literature, it often sounds as if the goal of the journey of awakening is to enter a state in which the separate self has completely dissolved, and there is a detached indifference to life because there are no separate individuals to care about. But this is not what I experience when I'm deep awake and living lucidly.

Being deep awake doesn't diminish my appreciation of the story of Tim; it enhances it. When I wake up to the depths of my essential nature, Tim doesn't disappear, he comes alive. I care more about life than I do in the normal waking state because, when I'm lost in my story, I tend to become numb just to cope with the suffering inherent in separateness.

If I'm lost in the story of Tim, I become fearful, selfish, and agitated. So I need to step out of the story and become conscious of my deeper identity, which is free, spacious, and at peace. But the process doesn't stop there. Now I'm ready to really engage with the story because I know that fundamentally all is well.

I used to see the goal of the adventure of awakening as a state of enlightenment, in which I dissolved into the oneness of things. But for me, being deep awake is a state of *both* transcendental enlightenment *and* passionate enlivenment. When I live lucidly, I am *both* conscious of oneness *and* in love with separateness.

Lost Tim and Lucid Tim

Coming up with the analogy between being deep awake and lucid dreaming was a breakthrough moment for me. I went on to write a little book called *Lucid Living* that encapsulated the essence of the philosophy I'm exploring with you in greater detail now. Since then I've found it much easier to take others into the deep awake state, as lucid living is a vivid and accurate description of the state of consciousness we inhabit when we wake up.

People often imagine that when we wake up to oneness, the experience of being a separate individual will somehow come to an end. But this isn't what happens, and when our individuality stubbornly refuses to disappear, we become confused. Once we see that the goal of awakening is to be conscious of *both* our separate identity as a person *and* our essential identity as awareness, it becomes much easier to wake up to oneness. And this is because we understand that we don't have to stop experiencing our separate self. We simply need to become conscious of our deeper being as well.

In one way, living lucidly changes nothing: life continues to be a mix of good and bad, pleasure and pain, joy and suffering. Yet in another way, living lucidly changes everything, because we have a new perspective on the challenges of everyday existence.

To illustrate this, I'd like to tell you about two people I know well: Lost Tim and Lucid Tim.

Lost Tim is selfish. He thinks that he's just a separate individual and needs to look after number one. He's generally kind to others because that's in his self-interest. But when the chips are down, compassion goes out the window. Unfortunately, this cuts him off from genuine love, so there's a hole in his soul that never gets filled.

Lucid Tim is the center of his own story, and he has to make sure that he takes care of his own needs. But he is also selfless, because he's conscious that his essential identity is one with all, so he wants to care for others. And this experience of big love heals his emptiness inside.

Lost Tim is very scared because he knows that truly terrible things could happen to him. This fear dominates his life. Sometimes it's just an underlying anxiety, but it's always there.

Lucid Tim has lots of frightening things to contend with in his life, too. But he's also conscious of his essential identity, which is always safe. This gives him the courage to engage with life as a daring adventure rather than a terrifying ordeal.

Lost Tim gets angry when people don't treat him as they should. He identifies with his separate identity, so he protects it when it's threatened. But this means that he's often agitated and craves peace.

Lucid Tim is sometimes abused by others and needs to protect himself as well. But he's accepting, even when he's also troubled, because he's conscious of his essential identity that is forever detached and serene. *Cannot be threatened*

Enjoying the Life-Dream

What a great movie! I've just been watching Wim Wenders's *Wings of Desire*. It's very slow, too long, and in German . . . on the face of it, not the ingredients for one of my favorite movies. But the themes explored by this film make it a masterpiece. It explores the world of the angels over Berlin, who are only glimpsed by the innocent eyes of children. But these are not angels as normally imagined. They are detached figures in long trench coats who witness the incoherent out-pouring of people's thoughts while comforting them in their distress. And they collect intense moments of life like little haiku poems. It's a haunting vision.

The angels are free from all of the struggles and suffering of being human. Yet they are alienated from the passion and pleasure of life, so Wenders films their world in black and white. The story follows a particular angel called Damiel, who fantasizes about how it would feel to actually taste a cup of coffee, be overcome by an emotion, or tell a lie. Eventually, Damiel's longing for visceral experience culminates in his falling in love with a woman . . . and he makes his decision.

The angel abruptly finds himself in the human world, along with a curious suit of armor, and the film bursts into radiant color. For me, this captures something important about living lucidly. Like the angel in the movie, to become enlivened I need to discard the protective suit of armor that isolates me from the pain and pleasure of existence. When I withdraw from life and simply witness what's happening, there's a detached serenity, but life can become colorless. It's only when I enter into the tumultuous passions and personal attachments of the human adventure that I come to life.

Wings of Desire explores the coexistence of the human and angelic worlds, and this affected my experience of watching the film. I became conscious that I was both a detached observer in the cinema and also a participant in the unfolding drama. I was safely outside of the story, but I was drawn into it by my fascination with the hero's dilemmas. This is a great analogy for what happens when I live lucidly.

I love it when a movie captivates my attention; however, I don't want to completely identify with the hero, since when the story becomes harrowing, I find it too disturbing. This rarely happens because I know that I am basically safe in the cinema. In the same way, waking up to my essential identity gives me a detached serenity from the trials and tribulations of the story of Tim. But just being detached would be like watching a movie and merely seeing colored patches projected on a screen. Where's the fun in that?

A movie is only enjoyable when I enter into the illusion, because then it moves and thrills me. Likewise, life only moves and thrills me when I enter into the illusion of separateness. Yet I don't want to be completely lost in the story of life any more than I want to be lost in a movie, as that would be hell. I want to *both* enter into the drama *and* have the tacit knowledge of being a detached observer.

I sometimes think that I want everything to go well for Tim. But I actually want the dramas of existence, because without them the story is bland and uninspiring. Who wants to watch a movie in which things start well, everything works out, and it all ends happily ever after?

What we really want is "safe danger," which is why we love the movies so much. And lucid living allows us to experience safe danger by entering into the thrills and spills of life with a fundamental sense of peace and security.

As a child, if a movie scared me I would pinch myself so that I'd remember I was in a cinema. For me, spiritual practices are a bit like pinching myself. When I've become so identified with the hero in the story of Tim that it has become terrifyingly real, I need to remember that everything is in fact okay. But when I know it's okay, I don't want to remain in a state of detached indifference. I want to get into the story again.

Paradoxically, I've found that the more I step out of the story of Tim, the more I'm able to really enjoy his adventures. When I'm lost in separateness, it's so frightening that I wear a psychological suit of armor to protect myself, which deadens me to life. I become scared and take refuge in numb insensitivity. Only when I know I'm truly safe can I risk diving into the whirling currents of the life-stream.

Watching *Wings of Desire* has made me appreciate that desire is the juice of life. And this makes me uncomfortable with some of the

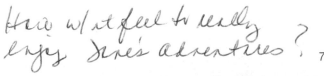
How w/ it feel to really enjoy Sine's adventures?

spiritual literature I used to admire so much, which portrays desire as something pernicious to be avoided. In my experience, desire is natural and necessary. Desire is only a problem when I'm so busy wanting things to be different that I don't appreciate the present moment. But when I'm lucid, I find myself *both* full of desire *and* free from desire. I am conscious of Tim, who wants things to get better, and my essential identity, which unconditionally accepts things as they are.

The turning point in the film comes when the angel, while toying with the idea of becoming human, is unexpectedly spoken to by the actor Peter Falk (best known as the star of the TV series *Columbo*). In *Wings of Desire,* Falk plays himself, but there's an unexpected twist because it turns out that he was once an angel. And now he wants to entice Damiel into the human world by enthusing about how wonderful it is to feel emotion and enjoy pleasure.

This has made me think about making some changes to my stand-up philosophy show. I usually concentrate on waking up to oneness, but really I want to entice people into consciously engaging with the dramas of the life-dream. I want us to know that we are one, and feel empowered to express our unique individuality by passionately playing our part in the story of life.

What I really want to say is this . . .

Each one of us is the hero of our own movie. Isn't that great?!

I'm a walk-on part in your movie. Other people get to play the romantic interest or comic sidekick. But you're the star who's in every scene.

Objectively, you're an insignificant speck of dust passing through this vast universe. But subjectively, you're the center of the universe, around which everything revolves.

You're the hero of this great drama, so why not live heroically? Why not be open to the possibilities of all you could be and everything you could experience? Why not dare to be fully human?

And the secret to daring to be really alive is to realize that life is like a movie, so you are fundamentally safe. In the movie there's laughter and tears, but everything is always okay . . . even during the scary parts.

Once you understand this, you can stop holding back and start to strut your stuff. You're the star of the show, so put in the performance of a lifetime!

But it's also important to remember that everyone is the star of the show from a different perspective. You need to play a positive part in other people's story lines, as well as inviting them to play a positive part in your story line. Then we'll all enjoy this adventure of life.

CHAPTER 8

AWAKENING THROUGH THE DREAM

I'm beginning to surface from a good night's sleep. Debbie is lying by my side, and I give her a gentle squeeze. Then I ask her playfully, "Where did this world suddenly come from? A few minutes ago, I was deep asleep and there was nothing. Now this 'Tim' fellow is back again."

Debbie is still semiconscious and unimpressed by being bothered with such a silly question. "Let's doze for a while," she suggests. But it's too late for me—I'm off into philosophical speculation. *What is deep sleep exactly?* I wonder to myself. *What is this strange state in which I exist but I don't know that I exist?*

And then it hits me . . .

The deep sleep state is the ocean of unconscious awareness, from which the dream of Tim arises every morning.

In the deep sleep state, I dissolve into this oceanic oneness, which is the ever-present ground of my essential being.

[handwritten: I am conscious as Jane]

In the waking state, my essential being arises as the mysterious presence of consciousness I call "I," which is witnessing Tim and his adventures.

In the deep sleep state, my essential being is a limitless nothing with the potential to be conscious of everything. It's the primal source of all.

A few minutes ago in deep sleep, I was unconscious, but now I'm experiencing an afterglow of this nebulous state . . . a visceral memory of blissful well-being and profound peace.

[handwritten: consciously]

[handwritten: I can stay conscious or go unconscious]

[handwritten: The path of focusing attention of meditating is similar to going to sleep]

As I focus my attention on the ground of my being, I begin to consciously enter the ocean of emptiness that I dissolve into unconsciously every night in deep sleep.

I feel spacious and free, and profoundly reassured that everything is okay. I'm immersed in timeless presence.

I'm deep asleep, but I'm also awake . . . I'm deep awake.

And this is making me realize something very obvious but extremely significant . . .

I can only enter the deep awake state because I'm conscious. And I'm only conscious because I'm experiencing separateness.

When I don't experience separateness, I'm in deep sleep. So this means that separateness is not an irrelevant illusion. It's a prerequisite for my being conscious at all.

If I wasn't conscious of appearing to be this separate individual called "Tim," I wouldn't be able to become conscious of my essential nature as the primal awareness, which is one with all.

Then Debbie says, "Damn it, we've overslept." And I suddenly remember that I've got a seminar to run today, so I'd better stop philosophizing and get my act together.

The Image in the Mirror

The razor removes the shaving foam and stubble from my face. Then, while I'm cleaning up my appearance to face the world, I notice my image looking back at me from the bathroom mirror. Who is that old-looking, bald-headed geezer? I'm heading for 50. How did that happen? The funny thing is that I still feel the same today as I did when I was 18. My body has aged and my personality has matured . . . a bit. But it feels as if my essential nature is exactly the same.

I stop shaving and look intensely at my eyes in the mirror. What I see are two colored circles, at the center of which is literally a hole. Where is the "I" who is looking through those holes? I can't see the "I" in the mirror because it's not a part of the appearances. It's the *I is* mysterious presence of awareness. This is my essential nature, which never changes.

Looking at my reflection is waking me up and insights are arising . . .

This image in the mirror isn't really who I am. He's just Tim's reflection.

And "Tim" isn't who I really am either. He is an image arising within awareness, like a character in a dream.

Without Tim, there would be no reflection, but without the mirror, Tim can't see himself. In a similar way, awareness is dreaming itself to be Tim so that it can see itself . . . experience itself . . . know itself.

So this Tim guy is pretty important . . . even if he is getting a bit decrepit these days.

Then I feel a sharp sting on my cheek. I've cut myself, and I'm bleeding slightly. When I don't pay enough attention to the appearances, it can hurt.

Consciousness Is Separateness

I'm in Northern Ireland to run a day seminar. I'm sitting in a circle of about 20 people in a light and spacious room, with magnificent views of the Mountains of Mourne. Des Rice built this room as an extension to his house in Newcastle a few years ago because he wanted to create a space where a group of people could gather to explore new ways of looking at life. He didn't know who these people would be when he built the place, but he felt sure that it would work out. And it has, as here we are, gathered together for me to present a day of philosophy. The first meeting in this amazing room.

I love being in Northern Ireland because I grew up in England watching the news about "the Troubles" here, and I always wanted to contribute something to the peace process. And now, in my own small way, I'm getting to do just that, helping people see through the separateness that divides us.

The gathering today is a fantastic mix of people from across the religious divide, brought together by their experience of waking up. We've got a couple of radical Catholic nuns, who are into an Earth-based spirituality that seems decidedly Pagan. And then there's a wonderful gentleman whom Des calls "the Buddha of Ballymena." Ballymena is a Protestant heartland, but "the Buddha" saw through sectarian divisiveness decades ago, after waking up while working in a bottling factory. He has a humble, openhearted, everyday authenticity that I find very appealing.

I've been talking for a while, so I invite the group to ask questions. The Buddha jumps in with a biggie:

"How can we be one with all?"

My answer is playful:

"That's easy. Just go to sleep, because in the deep sleep state, there is no separateness."

He looks perplexed and laughs, so I continue:

"I know that wasn't what you meant, but I want to make an important point. You see, I don't think that we want to be one with all; we want to be *consciously* one with all.

"And here's the thing: consciousness requires separateness. We're only conscious when we conceptualize the world into discrete things, including seeing ourselves as individual people. But the fact that we're conscious through separateness allows us to pay attention to our essential nature, which is one with all.

"We can't *only* be conscious of oneness, but we can *also* be conscious of oneness."

Then the Buddha says,

"So you're saying that separateness isn't a bad thing?"

And I reply,

"In the spiritual literature, separateness is sometimes dismissed as an irrelevant illusion, but it seems to me that the opposite is true. Separateness is absolutely necessary, because without it, we wouldn't be conscious at all.

"Conscious oneness is only possible because we're experiencing separateness. But we don't want to get so lost in the separateness that we aren't conscious of the oneness, as that leads to a lot of avoidable suffering. We need to be conscious that we are *both* separate *and* not separate."

Then the Buddha says,

"So when we wake up to oneness, the separateness doesn't magically disappear?"

And I reply,

"Exactly. And realizing this has made it a lot easier for me to wake up to oneness, since I'm not expecting the impossible. I spent years imagining that when I finally became enlightened, my experience of separateness would permanently dissolve into an ocean of oneness. This hasn't happened. And that's because I can't *only* be conscious of oneness. But I can *also* be conscious of oneness." *(As well as separate)*

Then the Buddha says,

"So you're saying that the goal of spirituality is to be conscious of both separateness and oneness at the same time?"

And I reply,

"Yes. That's lucid living. Our identity is characterized by polarity. Right now we are the oneness of the primal awareness dreaming itself to be all of these separate individuals sitting in this circle. In the normal waking state, we're conscious that we're separate. When we live lucidly, we're also conscious that we are one. And this changes how we see separateness.

"When we're lost in separateness, we view with suspicion, even horror, the differences between us. Other people's perspectives are a threat to our way of seeing things. But when we wake up to oneness, we see that the diversity of life is something to be celebrated."

Then the Buddha says,

"This is what people in Northern Ireland need to understand. We need to celebrate our differences, rather than fight about them."

So I add,

"People *everywhere* need to understand that we're both one and many. This is the only way we'll heal the divisions between us."

Connecting "I" to "I"

The young woman is trying to fight back the tears that are welling up in her eyes. It's the end of my seminar, and everyone is sitting silently in a tight circle. We're all looking at the young woman, who is slowly gazing around the circle and making eye contact with each of us in turn. But we're doing much more than just looking at each other eye to eye . . . we are connecting "I" to "I."

As the young woman's eyes meet mine, I see a beautiful face, full of character and kindness. But I also see through the veil of appearances to connect with her deeper identity, which I can't see or hear or touch. I am meeting the mystery of awareness, conscious through a different person. We are communing as one, and this is making us both feel emotional because it's an experience of big love.

Everyone in the room, in his or her own unique way, has already experienced what this young woman is experiencing now. One after another we've focused our collective attention on each individual, while that person has made eye contact with everyone . . . and connected "I" to "I."

This is an extremely powerful consciousness-raising exercise I devised to help people experience how good it feels to know that we are one awareness connecting with itself through the appearance of separateness. It's very simple and really works. We look at each other all the time and think nothing of it. But when we're lucid, this can be an opportunity to experience a profound communion.

The young woman closes her eyes, embarrassed that she's so tear-ful. But she needn't be, because the whole group is grateful to her for expressing the collective emotion that is filling the room. The atmosphere is charged. It's as if the air is heavy with vibrating energy. We are all vibrating together.

This is the completion of our time together, and we've arrived at our destination. I take the hands of the people on either side of me, and this ripples around the circle until we are all holding hands. Then I gently say,

"So here we are . . . living lucidly . . . conscious of being *both* separate *and* not separate.

"And it's because we are *both* separate *and* not separate that we can love each other.

"How cool is that?!"

There is general agreement that this is very cool indeed. And we sit there in the vibrating silence . . . one and many . . . bathing in big love.

When I run a seminar, my deepest desire is that we wake up to oneness and commune together in this experience of big love. Knowing that we are one is not a sterile realization. It is a vibrant emotion and a bodily feeling. It is a love that fills the hole in our soul and makes us feel complete. The adventure of awakening is a journey to the heart of love. (our own heart of love

The Importance of Choice

It's a beautiful morning and I'm walking in the Mountains of Mourne. I'm following a wooded path alongside a babbling brook, which cascades down to the sea. Every now and then I stop to catch my breath and enjoy the panoramic view. And the higher I climb, the more spectacular the view becomes.

While walking I'm thinking about the importance of "free will." It seems to me that human beings often think that they are acting freely, when actually they are merely reacting from their cultural conditioning. Here in Northern Ireland, for example, people on both sides of the conflict believe that they are choosing their positions. But in reality, how they think is simply a product of the particular culture they happened to grow up in.

We like to say that we're born free, but I'm not sure that's true. We're born with instincts that unconsciously govern our behavior, just as with other species. Then we become socialized by being conditioned into our cultural story. We have to learn to be free by becoming conscious of our instinctual responses and questioning our conditioning. Freedom is something that we achieve by becoming more conscious. Only when we are conscious enough to doubt our conditioning can we choose how we see things. Only when we are conscious enough to resist our habitual thought patterns can we choose how we react to a situation.

The more conscious I am, the more freedom I experience. It's like walking up this mountain. The farther up I go, the more I can see. When I become more conscious, I can glimpse more possibilities to choose between. In fact, sometimes my freedom seems so enormous that it's quite overwhelming. That's what the existentialist philosophers found.

But how does the experience of choice sit with the reality of oneness? When I'm deep awake, I can see that life is one stream of events in which there is no separateness. Everything is just happening naturally as an integral part of the flow of Tao . . . including Tim "choosing" this or that.

Does this mean that the experience of choice, which we humans hold so dear, is a meaningless illusion? Are we no more than organic automatons, reacting blindly to our environment? I don't think so. For me, knowing that all is one makes Tim's experience of choice seem even more important.

The primal awareness is unconsciously dreaming up the universe, and it becomes conscious through the individual beings it imagines itself to be. I am the primal awareness conscious through Tim. And so, through Tim, the primal awareness has the experience of conscious choice.

The primal awareness is doing everything, but mostly unconsciously. It is being this mountain unconsciously. It is being this brook and these trees unconsciously. But through Tim, it has consciously chosen to walk up the mountain and admire the view. The primal awareness has consciously responded to the world it has unconsciously created.

Conscious Evolution

Through the conscious choices of separate individuals, the primal awareness can consciously intervene in the otherwise unconscious process of its evolution. Most of the story of evolution has been deeply unconscious and therefore very slow. But when consciousness gets involved, things really speed up, as the short period of human history shows.

Evolution is the process of the primal awareness unconsciously imagining new possibilities in the dream of life, some of which are selected out as successful and others rejected. Human beings can consciously take part in this creative process. New possibilities arise from the unconscious depths of the imagination, and we choose those we wish to make manifest and those we don't. We are the universe consciously evolving.

Less-conscious forms of life have less choice in how they respond to the dilemmas of life as they arise. I was recently reading in a scientific journal about some birds in the north of England who nest near the sea. With the onset of global warming, the sea level is rising, and a large number of their nests were washed away last year. This year they've returned and nested in exactly the same place, so disaster is looming for this species.

Human beings are more conscious than these birds are, so we would soon realize that we needed to move home. But we're still unconscious enough to regularly behave in ways that could lead to our own destruction. That's why we need to make the next evolutionary jump by becoming collectively deep awake, because then we'll see new possibilities and choose to act with compassion . . . so that things get better, not worse.

Will we become more conscious quickly enough? Evolution has been full of surprises, so who knows? For me, the really important question is: what can I do to help? The answer is that I can choose to wake up to oneness. Then I can lucidly and lovingly engage with the dream of separateness. I can choose to be a member of the deep awake tribe that is arising on the new edge of evolution.

CHAPTER 9

PLAYING
WITH POLARITY

This is great fun. Beau and I are playing soccer. Well, that's not entirely true. We're actually desperately pressing buttons on the Xbox controllers in our hands, playing *virtual* soccer. And it's utterly amazing. You become the players and make the passes. You can manage your team and compete for trophies. There's a whole world in that box. I wish there had been games like this when I was a kid.

And then the philosopher takes over and I think to myself . . . , this whole virtual reality has been created from ones and zeros. It looks as if we're in a vast stadium shooting and scoring, but behind the vivid veneer, it's just a dance of opposites. It's much more fun to play the game than think about all that, of course. But if I wanted a deeper understanding of what is going on, I'd have to return to the fundamental polarity of the ones and zeros in the programming script.

Now my mind is racing with thoughts about polarity. . . . Life is not a computer-generated virtual reality, but they are comparable because our experience is also fundamentally structured by the play of polarity. I guess that is why when we invented computers, polarity was the obvious idea to employ.

Polarity structures the way we think, and the way we think defines what we experience. We define a thing as "this," not "that." We define an event as "now," not "then." We know ourselves as "self," not "other." Everything we experience is defined by a complex of polarities. When I first introduced my children to language, I read them picture books illustrating lots of polarities . . . up and down, big and small, inside and outside, boy and girl, day and night, naughty and nice . . . the list is endless.

What fascinates me is that a polarity is inherently paradoxical. The poles of a polarity are opposites. Up is not down. Down is not up. Yet these poles can only exist together. There can't be "up" without "down" or vice versa. You can't have one pole without the other. So a polarity is an apparent either/or duality and an essential both/and unity. This is what I call the "polarity paradox."

During my philosophical explorations of life, I've constantly come across paradoxical both/and polarities. Life is both a mystery and a story . . . we are both one and many . . . I am both a character in the life-dream and the life-dreamer. And I have come to realize that both/and thinking is the key to understanding the paradoxical human predicament.

The idea that life is based on polarity has been hanging around for a very long time. I first came across it as a teenager when I read the Tao Te Ching. One of its central themes is the polarity of yin and yang. Later I found the idea of polarity in Western philosophy, where it's talked about as a "dialectic." And later still in Gnostic Christianity, where a polarity is called a "syzygy."

The concept of polarity can be difficult to grasp because it's an abstract principle. I can point to examples of polarity, but I can't point to polarity itself. In this way, it's like a scientific law of nature. I can't point to $E = mc^2$ in nature, because nature doesn't contain any such laws. They are scientific formulas that underlie the way nature works. In the same way, "polarity" is a philosophical principle that underlies the way things are.

Life is predicated on a primal polarity that could be described with terms such as mystery and manifest . . . potentiality and actuality . . . oneness and separateness . . . life-dreamer and life-dream . . . *nirvana* and *samsara* . . . emptiness and form. The poles of this polarity seem to be a duality, but essentially they are a unity. Just as a dream and the dreamer seem to be a duality but are essentially one.

The concept of polarity is now the foundation of my philosophy. Previously I thought that reality was fundamentally an oceanic oneness, so separateness appeared to be an illusion. But now I see that reality is fundamentally a polarity. It is both oneness *and* separateness *unity* . . . emptiness *and* form . . . eternity *and* time. And I don't need to reject one pole, I need to embrace both.

Damn it! Beau has just scored . . . again. Normally we're pretty evenly matched, which makes for a good game. But I've been distracted by philosophy, so this time I've been soundly beaten. I guess when someone wins, someone else has to lose . . . that's polarity for you. Luckily I'm a good loser. But then, as my son enjoys reminding me, "Good losers are losers."

The Two Poles of Your Identity

In this book, we began by exploring how we start to wake up by simply stepping out of our story into the mystery of the moment. Then we looked at the practice of "being conscious of being conscious," and this led us to recognize our essential nature as the "I" of awareness, which is one with all. Having woken up to oneness, we've looked at how we can engage with the dream of separateness from this new perspective by living lucidly.

Now I want to invite you to practice a wake-up exercise that involves moving your attention between your apparent identity as a person in the world and your essential identity as the "I" of awareness so that you are conscious of both poles of your identity. Take your time with this and carefully examine the reality of the present moment:

Be conscious of your apparent identity as a person in the life-dream.

Then become conscious of being the "I" of awareness— witnessing a flow of colors, shapes, sounds, aromas, thoughts, and feelings. *(the world of the senses)*

Now carefully examine your apparent nature and your essential nature . . . and you will see that they form a polarity.

this *that*

As a person, you are a body . . . an object . . . a thing in the world.

As awareness, you are a spacious presence . . . a subject . . . a nothing within which the world is arising like a dream.

As a person, you exist within the life-dream.

As awareness, the life-dream is arising within you.

As a person, you exist in time.

As awareness, time exists in you, because "time" is the ever-changing appearances arising within awareness like a dream.

As a person, you are an individual with freedom of choice.

As awareness, all is one, and there are no separate individuals . . . everything is just happening.

Like two sides of the same coin, the two poles of your identity are opposites that exist together.

Freedom of Focus

It's a lovely sunny morning, which is rare in the cloudy U.K., so I'm eating my breakfast outside in the garden. And I've just noticed something obvious. Right now my eyes are focused on my glass of orange juice on the table in front of me. But I can also see the garden around me in my peripheral vision. Now I'm moving my head and focusing on the kids' trampoline, and the table is in my peripheral vision. My vision is simultaneously focused and peripheral. *foreground & background*

This has made me conscious of something just as obvious: A similar thing is going on with my attention. I'm focused on my thoughts right now, but I'm still conscious that I'm eating my breakfast, since the world remains present in my peripheral attention. And if I were now to focus my attention on eating my breakfast, my thoughts would fade into the background temporarily while I savored the food.

This is very interesting: I have a foreground and a background to my attention.

If I focus my attention on the deep awake state, the waking world goes out of focus. But the waking world is still in my peripheral consciousness, so I can bring my attention to it if I wish. And if I focus my attention on the waking world, I can keep the deep awake state in my peripheral consciousness, so I can return my focus to it when I want to. I am able to move the focus of my attention between the poles of my identity, while retaining the other pole in my peripheral attention.

When I live lucidly, I shift between these two perspectives. It's a state of dynamic balance. It's not a compromise in which I settle for a bit of both. It's more like a dance where I move between the extremes. It's a continual conversation between oneness and separateness. It's a bit like keeping my balance when riding a bike. I change where I put my attention in response to the bends and twists of the life-road.

So perhaps I need to refine my understanding of what living lucidly involves. I need to be conscious enough that when I focus on separateness, the knowledge of oneness remains in my peripheral consciousness. Then I can easily change my focus to the deep awake state when I choose to, and allow the waking world to be in my peripheral consciousness.

The goal of awakening is not some permanent fixed state. It is free-flowing attention that can focus wherever it needs to at the time. It is being liberated from bondage to my story, so my attention can move between focusing on the mystery of the moment and focusing on Tim's adventures in time. When I become deep awake, I see how free my attention really is, and I can focus on whichever pole of my identity I need to right now. That's living lucidly.

The Practical World

I'm meditating and I'm enjoying the bliss of being deep awake. I'm conscious of being a spacious presence within which the world is arising like a dream. Thoughts and sensations are coming and going in my peripheral attention, but my focus is on the stillness of my essential nature.

I don't get much time to sit still and do nothing these days, but when I do, I find that I slip immediately into a deep awake state, where I'm immersed in profound peace and well-being. I love it.

Then Debbie calls me to come downstairs, as our financial advisor is here to talk to me about the mortgage. I open my eyes and stretch my legs. It's been a wonderful meditation. As I go downstairs, I feel spacious and present, so when I greet my visitor, we connect immediately. This is such a nice way to be.

Now he's showing me figures about interest rates, but I'm much too spaced-out to understand what he's going on about. I've been deeply immersed in the oceanic oneness, and I'm finding it difficult to engage with the practicalities of separateness. I'd prefer to avoid thinking about my financial affairs because I don't want to get sucked into anxiety. When I'm in this big space, these things don't seem to matter. Money in particular always feels ridiculously absurd.

But this just won't do. I need to sort out the mortgage. I've got a family to house, for heaven's sake. So I concentrate on the numbers before me. As they start coming into focus, the experience of oneness—which had been in the foreground of my attention a few moments ago—fades into the background. Okay. I'm with it now. I can hear what he's saying about the mortgage, and it's good advice.

Eventually, the financial advisor departs. I sink my attention into the mystery of the moment, and my money worries fade into the background. Then I hear my kids coming home from school, and my focus moves again so that I'm ready to enjoy a role I really love . . . playful dad.

Passive and Active

I have found that the secret to living lucidly in the everyday world is having the freedom to move my focus from the deep awake state to the waking world and back again. Otherwise I become anxious or ineffective.

I find it interesting that during those periods of my life in which meditation has been my primary focus, I've not been particularly active or creative, just spacious and content. It's good to have times of withdrawal to become familiar with the deep awake state, but I don't want to stay there all the time.

I see this clearly when I'm writing. The creative process involves letting go into the inspirational world, where I dream up new ideas. But it also involves engaging with the practical world, where I express these ideas in particular patterns of words.

I love just hanging out in the inspirational state, but nothing much gets done. I've had endless creative visions that have come to nothing because of my unwillingness to shift my attention to the painstaking graft of the practical world. To be truly creative, I need to allow my focus to flow between these worlds.

Sometimes I'm reluctant to engage with the difficult world of doing because I don't want to forget the passive presence of being. But this is just as "one-sided" an approach to life as when I'm embroiled in the story of separateness.

When I live lucidly, my focus moves fluidly between the active and passive poles of my identity. And in my experience, this fluidity of focus is the way to enjoy a creative life as an active participant in the life-dream, while also bathing in the bliss of my deeper being. It is the secret of enlivenment.

A Journey to Lucid Living

Looking back on my life, I can see that my experience of being awake has changed and my understanding of the journey of awakening has evolved.

To begin with, I woke up sporadically in dramatic fashion and then found myself plunged back into separateness. This felt like a magical one-night stand with my soul mate, who then rushed off the next morning without leaving a phone number. It was the best moment of my life, but I was left with a big hole in my heart that could only be filled by the one and only.

I regularly experienced profound moments of becoming deep awake, but between them were periods of desolate confusion and heartbreaking longing. At one point I even took a line from T. S. Eliot's "Four Quartets" and inscribed it in large letters above my bed:

> "Ridiculous the waste sad time
> Stretching before and after."

I wanted out from my story and into the mystery. I was determined to do whatever it took to escape this crazy, mixed-up world and experience the bliss of big love. If that meant withdrawing from society and sitting cross-legged for hours staring at a white wall, then I was up for it. I even became celibate . . . but not for long.

Throughout this process, I saw myself as "Tim" on a spiritual journey toward enlightenment. Then I had the momentous realization that essentially I'm not a person, and everything changed. I suddenly saw that in the oneness of things, there never was a "Tim" to be enlightened or endarkened. My personal choices seemed unimportant, because there was "no doer." Things were just unfolding naturally of themselves.

The logic of what I was experiencing suggested that separateness was a meaningless fantasy and nothing really mattered. But this just didn't feel right. And when I became a father, my love of my family forced me to acknowledge that my personal life really mattered to me, and no amount of meditation or philosophy could convince me otherwise.

This is when I developed the idea of "lucid living," based on the analogy between the deep awake state and lucid dreaming. This gave me a way to understand how I could *both* wake up to oneness *and* engage with my everyday life. It helped me understand the polarity paradox at the heart of existence. And I came to see that separateness is a blessing, not a curse, for it is only through the experience of separateness that we can wake up to oneness.

When I started my journey, I wanted to step out of my story and be immersed in the ecstatic mystery. Then I discovered my essential nature as the "I" of awareness, so I wanted to reject separateness and dissolve into the impersonal oneness. But I've come to see separateness as something to be celebrated. These days I see myself as an individual expression of the primal awareness who is choosing to live lucidly, by *both* being conscious of my essential nature as the primal awareness *and* engaging passionately with the adventures of Tim.

Recognizing the polarity of my attention has led me to further refine my understanding of my spiritual goal. It seems to me that I need to be free enough to focus my attention wherever it feels appropriate, without becoming stuck anywhere. My goal isn't a fixed state of consciousness; it's being conscious enough to change my focus in response to my unfolding life experience. And it's when I can do this that I live lucidly in the everyday world. This is a state of *both* enlightenment *and* enlivenment, in which I experience the bliss of big love and the warmth of personal affection.

Throughout my adventures, love has always been the most important thing in my life. It was the all-embracing love I felt as a boy on the hill that made me begin my journey of awakening. It was the personal affection I felt as a father that led me to embrace separateness. It is the unconditional compassion I'm feeling right now that makes me want to serve humanity, by contributing to the creation of a deep awake world. For me, it's love that makes life worth living. Only love fills the hole in my soul.

CHAPTER 10

BIG LOVE

I'm sitting in a room sparkling with candles, and poignant music is playing quietly. Around me is a peaceful circle of people with their eyes closed. Through the windows, my gaze reaches out into the stillness of the night. Outside these walls is Chalice Well Garden, a magical sanctuary nestled below the Tor in my hometown of Glastonbury. I'm running a weekend seminar here, and we've just completed an initiation meditation that I've devised to help people experience the deep awake state.

An initiation is usually thought of as the beginning of something, and so it is. But in the ancient world, an initiation was seen as a glimpse of the goal toward which we are traveling. I see our initiation tonight as an opportunity to taste the reality of oneness and the ecstasy of big love. Then when we return to our everyday lives after the seminar, we will have a clear idea of where our journey of awakening is leading.

Up until this point, there have been a lot of ideas, along with some simple, practical exercises to help us see through separateness to our shared essential nature. I've kept things as playful as possible so that we can lighten up. But when it comes to this initiation, I ask people to find a deep seriousness and sincerity.

Whenever possible, I like to lead this initiation after sundown because there's something magical about the night. I prepare a beautiful space that opens the heart, and I ask everyone to enter in silence and sink into the stillness. I wait while the poignant music massages away the tensions in our souls. Then I begin a meditation in which we slowly explore and embrace the present moment with big love.

We become conscious of listening with love. We become conscious of the feelings in our bodies with love. We become conscious of the sensation of breathing with love. We become conscious of thinking and imagining with love. Until we become conscious of our deeper nature, which *is* love. And then we dissolve into the mystery of the moment together.

I've just finished leading this meditation for the group of beautiful people now sitting serenely around in the vibrating silence, and the room is thick with big love. Everyone can feel it, and some people are emotional. No one wants to speak in case it breaks the enchantment of this precious place. Occasionally someone attempts a few words . . . "bliss" . . . "connection" . . . "enlightenment." A young woman sings a sweet song, and then we sink into the silence again.

As I look around me at all of these gorgeous faces, I celebrate our individuality. We are all one and yet so unique. Tonight we have among us a physicist, an artist, a retired businessman, a diplomat who speaks five ancient languages . . . and a transvestite named Colin. And in this oneness, we can delight in the differences. That wise gentleman over there is a priest in the Church of England . . . and he's sitting next to a wonderful lady who is a Wiccan high priestess!

No one wants to break the circle, so I'm beginning to wonder if anyone will ever go home. But eventually, one by one, the members of the group embrace before they leave, and our quiet party fades away. I lock the door of our meeting room and wander alone into the moonlit garden. In the black-and-white light of the night, I appreciate the rich textures of the flowers that surround me, and I sit by the Chalice Well and drop loose petals into the water.

It feels like fairyland. I've returned to the secret garden I frequented as a child. I'm drunk with love and overwhelmed by gratitude. To be in love with one person is sweet. To be in love with all is indescribable.

It is a love so deep that it has no end. I've often made this pilgrimage to the sacred temple of love that lies at the heart of the secret garden . . . and it feels like home.

Lust, Affection, Compassion

I'm feeling open and present today because I'm listening to some great music while I'm writing, and there's nothing like music to take me into a big love space. At the moment I'm letting the computer pick tracks at random from a playlist on iTunes I've created called "Big Love Songs." It's mainly old stuff that reminds me of times I've been loved-up in the past. I've just heard the charmingly naïve "What the World Needs Now Is Love," by Bacharach and David. Now I'm singing along to "One" by U2 and we've just arrived at my favorite line, about how we are one but not the same . . . so we get to carry each other.

We love someone when we see that we are two and one at the same time, so we connect through the separateness. I love my children because I feel one with them. They are separate individuals, but the veneer of separateness between us is transparent. Their joys are my joys. Their suffering is my suffering. Their dreams are my dreams.

There are songs on this playlist that relate to the whole spectrum of experiences we call "love," from universal compassion through personal affection to animal lust. Each of these loves is really about transcending separateness. Lust is the most basic love, when two bodies become one. A deeper sense of oneness arises with personal affection, since someone becomes such an important character in our story that it mitigates our awful isolation. But the deepest sense of oneness arises with transpersonal big love.

The greater love doesn't diminish the lesser; rather, it includes and completes it. Lust without personal affection is only a temporary respite from separateness. But personal affection can include lust, allowing us to playfully express our animal nature within the safety of human connection. Personal affection is wonderful, but it breaks down when our individual neuroses clash, unless we can also hold each other within the unconditional acceptance of big love.

Now Whitney Houston is belting out "The Greatest Love of All" from my speakers, and I'm flying. Over the years my understanding of life has constantly changed, but one simple conviction has remained: *all that really matters is love.* And I feel, somewhere deep inside, that we all know this. There is nothing better than to be in love with life . . . and only love can heal our heartbreak when we're hurting.

Loving Relationships

I'm in Buenos Aires as a guest speaker at a Oneness Summit, which is being run by an amazing organization called Humanity's Team. I'm sitting on the stage with some extraordinary people who have also been speaking at this event. We're doing a collective Q-and-A session, and a woman in the audience has just asked a great question:

> "I like the idea of spreading oneness and love in the world, but to be honest I find it hard just to be loving in my marriage. Why is this so difficult?"

This has touched a nerve, and the audience claps. This woman's question has reminded everyone of the challenges we all face in our personal relationships. There's a pause because none of the speakers wants to take this question, so I decide to jump in:

> "Perhaps I can attempt to answer your question from personal experience. I've been married twice. I messed up my first marriage, but I feel I'm not doing too bad with the second. The difference has been how I have understood love.

> "Love happens when we connect as one. When we're lost in separateness, we crave love to ease our isolation, but we go about things the wrong way. We attempt to be one with our lover by subsuming them within our personal self. But this is disastrous because it's precisely on the personal level that we're separate, and we need to honor this.

"When I see 'you' as an extension of 'me,' I end up trying to control you and mold you to fit into my world. And this is often how we treat our lovers, children, and friends. But it never works, as sooner or later the other person refuses to neatly fit into our story, and the relationship breaks down.

"This is what happened in my marriage to my first wife, Caroline. Looking back I can see that in many ways, I wanted to subsume her identity into Tim's identity, and eventually she just wasn't having it anymore. But this was a great learning experience because I've been able to avoid doing this in my second marriage to my wife, Debbie.

"As I've gotten older, I've found that the communion I crave doesn't lie in expanding my separate self to include another. It lies in transcending separateness altogether, so we embrace each other in unconditional big love. Understanding this means that I don't try to subsume 'Debbie' into 'Tim.' I recognize that we are essentially one but also separate individuals, so I respect and nurture her individuality.

"I've found that all the conflicts in my relationships arise because I'm lost in the story of Tim. And this means that when someone doesn't go along with my story, we argue. But if I'm awake to the mystery, I'm able to see the situation from other perspectives. I can try to understand someone else's story rather than clinging resolutely to my own.

"When I'm lost in separateness, I connect with someone only through my idea of who that person is in my story. And this means that there's always a subtle sense of alienation. The truth is, we can only authentically commune in the mystery of the moment. So it seems to me that when it comes to personal relationships, it's big love or bust!

"Having walked through the fire of countless personal conflicts, I've learned that the only real solution to division is the unity of big love. To make our personal relationships really work, we need to become deep awake. And it feels to me that the conflicts we experience are pushing us to become more conscious. Our loving relationships are the arena in which we can learn what love truly is."

The audience claps appreciatively, which I acknowledge with a smile. Then I pass the microphone back to the MC, who leans over to whisper playfully in my ear,

"You know, Tim, if the philosophy thing doesn't work out for you, I think you've got a great future in marriage counseling."

And this makes me laugh, for I suspect that Debbie would have serious reservations about my suitability for the job.

A Family Conflict

My father and I have ended up arguing. We've always been close, which makes it painful when we clash. I love and respect him because he's been a great dad who has always supported all my crazy endeavors. But today I'm struggling to connect with him. He seems closed off and difficult to reach. Our stories about life are so different that we sometimes just irritate each other.

And that's when it hits me. I see myself as the good guy here, but actually I'm completely lost in my story. If I wasn't, I wouldn't be arguing like this. I've learned that the test of whether I'm awake is to ask myself if I'm being loving. If I'm not being loving, I'm not awake, no matter how much I try to convince myself otherwise. And the truth is, I'm not being loving right now.

I can see that my dad is also lost in his story. But I've learned that it doesn't matter what state others are in; it matters what state I'm in. Just as when two people are pulling taut a piece of string, it only takes one person to let go for the tension to end.

Looking at this situation with new eyes, I see that my dad is imprisoned in his story like a cage—but rather than set him free, I've been rattling his cage, which has made matters worse. I feel as if I'm watching my dad's deeper self fading away behind the noise of our conflict and calling out plaintively for my help.

Then I realize that I need to stop talking and just give him a hug, so he knows how much I really love him. The problem is that I feel paralyzed because I can't let go of my story in which I'm right and he's wrong. But the price of this self-righteousness is too high. I can't bear the awful sense of separation. So, with an act of will, I get up and embrace him. And suddenly we are free together in love, and our stories are of no consequence.

Corner-Shop Communion

I've gone down to the local corner shop to buy a paper, and I'm casually chatting to the young woman behind the counter about how bad the weather has been lately. It's a trivial conversation to pass the time while she's getting me my change. But something profound is also happening. Behind the social niceties, I'm communing with someone whose name I don't even know.

As we chat together, I'm silently acknowledging the enormity of her deeper being. And as I do so, she is changing. She's stopped avoiding eye contact. Her face has softened, because she's smiling. We're totally present with each other. Then I take my paper and leave her serving the next customer, with whom she is now talking warmly.

As I walk home, I'm thinking about how my state of consciousness affects the way I relate to people. If I'm lost in the story of Tim and go to buy something from the corner shop, I see the woman who serves me as a "shop assistant," since that is her role in my story. If I'm more awake, I'm conscious that she is also a person full of hopes and fears, and this makes our meeting warmer and kinder. If I'm deep awake, I see all of that and more. I realize that I'm meeting the mystery made manifest in this unique form. And there's the opportunity to peek out from behind the veil of appearances and say "Hi."

That's what happened with the shop assistant today. We met in the moment. For this to happen, I didn't need to come in with "Good morning, mystery made manifest, I'd like to buy a paper please," as that would have freaked her out. I simply needed to be in the deep awake state and give her the space to join me should she wish to. And, as so often happens, this led to an unexpected moment of communion with a total stranger.

To love each other personally takes time. We need to talk to each other and share experiences. We need to laugh and suffer together. But to meet in the transpersonal oneness, we don't need to know each other personally at all. The connection from being to being is immediate and always possible. And whenever we commune in big love, it sends ripples of kindness out into the world.

Practicing Loving

If love is the most important thing in life, then it's worth practicing opening our hearts to love. This is why I'm experimenting with a little guided meditation I've devised that is based on a Buddhist technique called *Metta Bhavana,* which means "loving kindness." And I'd like to invite you to try it with me.

LOVING SOMEONE CLOSE

First, I'm going to take myself into a loving space by focusing on someone I find it very easy to love. I could choose one of my kids or a close friend, but I think I'll go for Debbie.

I'm evoking how good it feels when I know how much I love her. I'm remembering times we have shared that have been particularly loving. And now I'm going to allow myself to bathe in these warm feelings for a few minutes.

LOVING A STRANGER

Next I'm going to bring to mind a stranger to whom I'm indifferent. I think I'll choose the mail carrier. I don't have any particular feelings toward him because we've never talked.

I'm thinking about the mail carrier, and I'm making conscious the fact that he is a sentient being, just like me, who is experiencing all the joys and sufferings of life. I'm remembering that even my best friends were once strangers like this person is now.

I'm opening my heart and embracing the mail carrier with loving kindness. I'm imaginatively connecting with his deepest being where we are one.

LOVING SOMEONE I HAVE EXILED FROM MY HEART

Now for something more demanding. I'm going to bring to mind someone I find it difficult to love. I think I'll choose someone I've exiled from my heart because we've quarreled.

This is difficult because I keep feeling blame and judgment, not loving kindness. But I'm doing my best to let those feelings go and gently work to bring down the barriers that keep my heart closed.

I'm remembering how easy it is for all of us to act badly and that everyone has their side of the story. I am reaching through the separateness to this person's deeper identity, which is all goodness and crying out to be recognized.

Gradually, feelings of loving kindness are beginning to replace anger and resentment. And I feel much better for that.

LOVING MYSELF

Now I'm ready for the big one. I'm bringing to mind "Tim" so that I can embrace myself with loving kindness. This is the most difficult part of the exercise because there's so much about myself that I don't like.

But I'm trying to let go of self-criticism and reach out to myself with compassion, as if I were comforting a close friend or intimate lover. I'm wishing Tim well. I'm honoring what is good in Tim and forgiving him for his failings. I'm conscious of his essential goodness. I'm loving him unconditionally as he is.

LOVING THE WAY THINGS ARE

I'm feeling deep awake now. So I'm finally going to bring to mind the whole world. I'm imagining all that is going on right now. All of the laughter and pain, kindness and cruelty, beauty and ugliness. And I'm embracing things just as they are.

I rejoice at the joy and feel compassion for the suffering. I am conscious that, despite how bitter life can be, it's also very sweet. And I find myself in love with this moment in all of its poignant glory. It is a mystery beyond my comprehension.

Now I'm immersed in big love, and I'm going to stay here for a while. I feel at peace. I'm conscious of my deepest being, which is one with all. I am loving *being*.

Famous among Angels

I've sat down with my mum for a cup of tea because I need to ask her a very important question. We're very close, but we don't talk that much, since we don't need to. I love her so much it's impossible to express. She would describe herself as a very ordinary woman, but I think she's the most amazing person I've ever met.

My mum is an angel. Everyone loves her, because she loves everyone. She's in her 80s, and she's had cancer three times and a cerebral aneurysm—but she's still bouncing with energy, which she expends in unself-conscious service of all those around her. While I write books about oneness, she just gets on with being unconditionally kind, as if it were the most obvious thing in the world. She doesn't think about philosophy; she just seems to know it all anyway . . . without even knowing that she knows it.

It's my mum who inspired in me the desire to be of service to others. For me, love is the deep source of compassionate action that naturally springs from an open heart. Love is willingly putting others first; yet this is not selfless denial, since the joy of service is so much richer than selfish gratification. And I've learned all of this from watching my mum.

Years ago I realized something that shocked me at the time. I'd traveled the world in search of enlightened sages, but my real teacher had been right before me for all of my life. I thought that I needed to become some sort of holy man, but in that moment I knew my deepest aspiration was to become more like my mum.

It's remembering this that has prompted me to sit her down for tea so that I can ask my important question, for if I leave it any longer it may be too late. I want to know the secret of her continual buoyancy, even in the face of terrible suffering. But she doesn't know what I mean, since she doesn't analyze life like I do. So I ask her to think about it. At last, she says,

> "When I start feeling down, I just look around for someone who needs my help, and then I feel much better."

It's so simple that my mind goes quiet. Then I hear in my imagination the strains of a song I wrote for my mother when she had cancer, called "Famous among Angels." I liked the idea that, while the rich and glamorous are famous among men, the angels had never heard of any of them. Those famous among the angels are people who are just naturally kind and awake and unnoticed . . . like my mum.

CHAPTER 11

MEANING
AND MAGIC

Debbie and I have invited some new friends over for a meal. The conversation has inevitably come around to the "How did you two meet?" question. It's a great story, so I don't mind telling it. . . .

Debbie had been left while pregnant by the boyfriend she'd been with since she was 16. Luckily, some friends of mine, Sean and Angie, invited her into their home, where she gave birth to Beau. This was just down the road from where I was living, in the manor house by the church near Glastonbury. Sean and I were making music together at the time, so he would visit me in the studio and talk about this beautiful woman and her newborn baby who were staying with him. But Debbie and I didn't meet then, because she ended up returning to her birthplace, miles away in Hemel Hempstead.

A short time after this, the girlfriend I was with left me for another shaven-headed musician named Tim . . . only he was a lot more successful! The breakup was a painful reminder of the end of my marriage some years earlier. I was feeling grim, and Sean offered to cheer me up with a ticket to the World of Music and Dance festival.

I went to the festival, but it didn't cheer me up. I decided to leave, and on my way out I ran into Sean, who was going to meet Debbie and Beau, whom he'd also invited along. We reached the gate just as Debbie arrived, and when I saw this stunningly attractive woman, I instantly decided that I'd stay after all!

I offered to buy her a drink while she looked for a place to change Beau's diaper. And then I heard a familiar voice call my name. I looked around and there, among the thousands of festivalgoers, was my ex-wife, Caroline, whom I hadn't seen for years since our divorce. This was a shock, but it felt strangely perfect, because life had become dreamlike ever since I had laid eyes on Debbie and Beau.

I had the feeling that I should not ignore this extraordinary coincidence, so I decided to take some time with Caroline. She apologized for dragging me away from the pretty woman, but joked that she had perhaps saved me from another disastrous marriage. We talked together for an hour or so, and it was an intensely healing conversation in which we both felt forgiving and forgiven.

I returned to Sean and the party of people he had invited to the festival, feeling cleansed of the hurts of my past and much more positive. It soon became apparent that Sean had invited Debbie along because he wanted to set her up with a friend of his whom he'd also invited. But Debbie was now surrounded by a whole group of interested guys . . . and I was one of them.

In the short time we were chatting together, I realized that I was uncontrollably falling in love with this elegant woman's natural beauty and unaffected humility. And stranger still, I was falling in love with little Beau, whom I felt I'd known for lifetimes.

I wanted to be alone with Debbie so that we could really connect, but there was such a big party of us that it seemed impossible. So I did something that may sound silly and superstitious. I spoke to the universe and asked for a favor. I said,

> "If there's any good karma left in my 'karma bank,' I want to cash it in tonight. Please let me spend the evening alone with this gorgeous woman."

And . . . what d'you know? A short while later, Debbie and I found ourselves caught up in the swirling crowds of festivalgoers and became separated from our group of friends, whom we never found again all night. I knew then, with unshakable conviction, that we would be married, that I would be Beau's dad, and that Debbie and I would have a child together ourselves.

I enjoy telling the story of how I met Debbie and Beau because it was a very important day in my life. But I also find it interesting because it's full of seemingly meaningful coincidences. Was it just chance that I healed my first marriage and began my second marriage at the same time? It could be happenstance, but for me it was significant.

In my experience, the more lucid I am and the more dreamlike life becomes, the more "synchronicities" become commonplace. I have the intuitive conviction that I'm glimpsing a pattern underlying the apparent chaos. And I find that I can interpret my life as I would a dream, finding meaning hidden in the unfolding dramas.

When I'm deep awake, I feel enchanted by the magic of life. It's as if there's an ongoing conversation between the inner world of my soul and the events that happen to me. And in some strange way, they are like reflections of each other. Often life is dumb, and I can't understand what she is saying. Other times she's eloquent, and I hear her loud and clear . . . as on the day I fell in love with Debbie and Beau.

Most people who are on the journey of awakening have similar stories of meaningful moments in what seems to be the accidental warp and weft of life. At such times, we connect with the meaningful dimension of existence and see that the flow of our lives, like a dream, is telling us something.

The Symbolic Universe

I've been living in this amazing old gatehouse while I've been writing the book *The Jesus Mysteries* with my friend Peter Gandy. This was once where the monks from Glastonbury Abbey used to come to grind corn. I love living in the country because the stars are so much brighter without the light pollution of the town. Tonight they seem particularly radiant.

I'm lying on my back in the garden, staring up at the glittering sky, and I'm lost in wonder. I always find that contemplating the night sky takes me into the mystery. I can't get my head around the fact that the universe goes on forever. But neither can I imagine it coming to an end. And I certainly can't begin to comprehend Einstein's idea of curved space, which suggests that if I keep going long enough, I'll end up back where I already am.

Science has given us an extraordinary understanding of this marvelous spectacle, which blows my mind. But it can't begin to explain why it's so beautiful. A clever monkey doesn't need to find the universe awesome . . . but I do.

If I look at the universe with scientific objectivity, I see matter forming itself into vast balls of exploding chemicals in a chilling void, without meaning or purpose. But when I'm lucid, as I am tonight, I can also see this magnificent light show with the appreciative eyes of the poetic imagination. And then it seems full of meaning, like some extravagant dream.

I'm looking at the moon right now, glowing impassively in the darkness. Mystics throughout history have seen the sun and moon as natural symbols for our essential nature and our personal identity. The sun burns so brightly that our eyes can't look directly at it. But the moon has no light of its own and only shines because it reflects the glory of the sun. And it waxes and wanes, just as the body matures and then declines with age. The moon really is a great symbol for the personal self. It even has a face!

The ancients viewed the universe as a grand symbolic myth, full of hidden significance. And some of the strange coincidences about the sun and moon that Peter has been telling me about recently make me inclined to take this seriously. For example, the sun is 400 times the size of the moon. And yet, because the sun is 400 times farther away from Earth than the moon, they appear to be the same size. The odds against such an occurrence must be extremely high. And there's a further "coincidence" whose odds must also be astronomical . . . literally.

The moon occasionally passes in front of the sun because the orbit of the moon coincides with the path of the sun across the sky. And it's only because the heavenly paths of the sun and moon happen to coincide that we witness one of the most awe-inspiring cosmic events . . . a total eclipse.

Without the combined effect of these two extraordinary coincidences, eclipses would never happen. But then, life on our planet is the result of so many "coincidences" that the eminent astrophysicist Sir Fred Hoyle concluded that it must be a "put-up job."

Until relatively recently, most of humanity believed that the heavenly bodies, like all bodies, must have souls. Sir Isaac Newton imagined that the "attraction" between the souls of the planets must be the source of that force that we now call gravity. It was this force of attraction, he postulated, which bound all things together into a unity. We might equally call this unifying attraction by the name "love," as did Dante, who wrote about "the love that moves the sun and the other stars."

Materialist scientists eventually dropped Newton's term "attraction" and went instead for the word "gravity." It sounded more "rational" than the poetic idea that the cosmos might be a living being and that things might naturally be "attracted" to one another. And so living attraction became lifeless gravity . . . love became death.

This has left us in a universe in which the "heavenly bodies" no longer have souls. The glorious moon, the mysterious planets, and the bountiful earth are mere lumps of rock spinning through a meaningless void. But I can't live in that prosaic cosmos. Not because I can't face reality, but because this vision of the way things are is not real enough. It's missing the poetic dimension of existence, which can't be measured but only appreciated.

The Battle of the Baldies

It's my final year at university, and I'm driving to the train station to pick up my girlfriend, Caroline. I feel very awake because I've just completed a five-day retreat alone in my student apartment, fasting, meditating, and practicing Tai Chi Chuan. I have Gandhi's autobiography in my coat pocket because I've been studying his ideas about nonviolent resistance. And I've just shaved my head for the first time, which makes me look like a Buddhist monk.

As I walk up from the parking lot to the station, I see a lanky skinhead with an entourage of smaller youths who are harassing an elderly man in a suit. Once they notice me watching them, they start calling out abuse. Suddenly the big guy runs over to stand right in front of me, followed by his motley crew, who circles me aggressively.

Then he demands, "Do you want a smack in the mouth?" I reply, "No thanks." Unfortunately, it wasn't a yes-or-no question. What he meant was, "Do you want a smack in the mouth or would you prefer a head butt?" . . . so I get the head butt.

It's as if time has slowed, as his bald head rises up and descends violently onto my bald head. And as I collapse on the floor, all of the skinheads begin to yell and start to kick me. But I feel strangely fearless and in love with the moment. I'm relaxed and there's no anger. Then the most unexpected thing happens.

The gang of skinheads begin to fight among themselves. Each is telling the other to "F*ck off out of the way," because there's not room for all of them to have the pleasure of kicking me. Now their argument has turned into a full-blown brawl. And as they start to throw punches at each other, they move away from me altogether. So I stand up and walk calmly toward the station.

I make my way to the men's restroom, where I watch in the mirror as, cartoonlike, a huge bump rises above my left eyebrow. Then I meet Caroline and we drive home. As I leave the station, I spot the big skinhead, who is now on his own because his pack of friends has left on a train. Our eyes meet for a moment, and he seems alone and frightened. His bravado is gone, and my heart reaches out to him.

I feel very lucky to have escaped with just a black eye, but I wonder if it's luck or if the situation changed because of my state of consciousness. I've studied Tai Chi Chuan for years. Today I saw it in action because I overcame the situation by yielding to it. The power of my attackers turned against them. I saw Gandhian nonviolence in practice. And this all occurred because I was deep awake. I find it fascinating how my state of consciousness can shape my experience. And how it always feels as if life is trying to teach me something.

The Message of the Mamas

Magic works. There's no doubt about it. The evidence is here before my eyes. Last week I was a penniless musician with a fanciful vision of having a professional 24-track recording studio in which to record an album of softcore dance music with my lifelong friend Theo Simon. Today I'm sitting in that very studio, marveling at all of the flashing lights and dials before me. And at the bizarre series of events that has led me here.

I'm in my early 30s and obsessed with how music can change consciousness. A few weeks ago, Theo and I watched a BBC documentary called *From the Heart of the World,* about the Kogi Indians of Colombia. This mysterious tribe, led by shamans called "Mamas," had recently decided to communicate with the rest of the world. Calling themselves the "Elder Brothers," they issued a dire warning to us Westerners . . . the "Younger Brothers": our way of life is killing Mother Earth, and we are heading for environmental catastrophe.

Theo and I were very moved by this message, so we decided to help bring the Mamas' warning to the world by making a dance album called *MotherGroove,* accompanied by a music video with a strong environmental message. When we contacted the director of the Kogi documentary, he said that he would support us . . . as well as enigmatically cautioning, "If you get involved with the Mamas, expect the unexpected."

Neither Theo nor I could have predicted what happened next. Bizarrely, we had both married sisters in the same family . . . Caroline and Natalie . . . and even more bizarrely, they left us at the same time. We were feeling raw and vulnerable. We took refuge in our Kogi project, but things weren't looking good because neither of us had any money to finance our vision.

I was clearly distressed about the end of my marriage, so a friend suggested that I stay at the New Age center he owned in Spain to give me time to think. My visit coincided with a course being run on "the power of intention." I was already in an altered state and very open, so I threw myself into the course with passion.

The essential idea we explored was that we can magically shape what happens to us by clearly framing our intentions. I knew from previous experience that this could work . . . so I gave it a go. I dreamed my wildest dream: I imagined myself in a manor house in the country with a fully equipped 24-track studio, making my album and music video. To begin with, it seemed like an impossible fantasy, but the more I allowed myself to dream, the more real it became for me.

When I returned home, I was charged up with my vision, but I still had no idea how to make it a reality. A few days later, however, I received a call from a friend who was very enthusiastic about what I wanted to do. She had set up a meeting for Theo and me with a couple who ran a consciousness-raising, Earth-centered organization called the Solar Trust.

We soon found ourselves in a magnificent home overlooking the sea, with a distinguished-looking gentleman and his wife, who was confined to a wheelchair. These people were wealthy, and sympathetic to our vision. Not long after we left, we received a call from the gentleman telling us that he would finance everything . . . and for quite an extraordinary reason: his wife was a medium, and she'd received messages from spiritual beings called the Els, telling her that it was very important to support our work.

I don't know who these Els are, but I like them—because here we are, installing a 24-track mixing console in a manor house in the country, just as I envisioned. It sounds improbable, but this is really happening.

A newspaper wanted to do a feature on our project, and I made the naïve mistake of telling them this story. They printed a full-page picture of me, along with the headline: Musician Given Money by Elves.

That's the media for you! It sounds crazy enough with Els, let alone elves, but somehow I do seem to have manifested my vision of taking the message of the Kogi Mamas to the world.

Lucid Magic

I've found that the more lucid I am, the more the line between my inner world and the outer world becomes blurred—I no longer experience them as separate, and my fantasies become reality. My intentions shape the way the dream of life unfolds. This is what the ancients called "magic."

The magical power of thought became really obvious to me in my early 20s, when I joined a small group of young people studying occultism and Kabbalah. During this time, life became outrageously dreamlike. I found myself permanently inhabiting another reality in which odd things happened all the time. Even the way this adventure started was quite incredible.

I'd just come back from my first trip to India, where I'd met some Indian occultists who'd interested me. I was meditating at my parents' home and fixated on the intention that I would work with a real magician because I wanted to actually experience magic, not just read books about it.

The next morning I received a call from my friend Peter Gandy, who was studying at Cardiff University at the time. He'd "accidentally" met a mysterious young occultist in an arts center and kept raving enthusiastically about having found the keys to understanding the universe. I got on the train for Cardiff the same day to meet the "magician."

On the first night, the three of us went out walking in the night, discussing the ancient Egyptian deities and their occult significance. We began to talk about the god Horus, symbolized by a hawk, and the goddess Isis, symbolized by an owl. At that moment an owl hooted, and we looked up into the sky. The clouds had formed the unmistakable shape of a hawk's head, with the full moon perfectly placed as the Eye of Horus.

This was the beginning of a yearlong adventure studying magic, which left me with a boxful of strange experiences. I rarely talk about them because they sound so kooky. I don't want to become associated with the superstitious baloney that gets passed off as spirituality. As a philosopher, I pride myself on being skeptical, but I can't deny that on many occasions my intentions have manifested as realities, and this has driven me to explore how and why this happens.

Big Self and Small Self

I'm chatting with my son, Beau, who is now seven years old. I enjoy our conversations because he's a natural philosopher, so what he says often surprises me and gets me thinking. Today we've been talking about ghosts and whether they can walk through walls. I've just asked him if he knows why it is *he* can't walk through walls . . . and his response is not what I expect:

> "I touch the wall with my hand, but it can't go through because someone has imagined it so well it's become a wall."

I'm intrigued, so I ask what he means. He tells me:

> "We've all got our imaginations together to imagine the world."

I grab a pen and start jotting down what he's saying, since the natural insights of children fascinate me. Then I decide to push him to explain how we "imagine" the world together. And he replies in an offhand way:

> "My big self imagines everything. My big self is the universe. My small self is Beau."

I wonder if he understands what he's saying. I want to find out, but he's wandered off to play on the computer.

Creating Reality

When we dream lucidly, we can influence what happens in our dream. We don't suddenly find ourselves in complete control of everything that occurs because then we wouldn't be dreaming at all; we'd be having a waking fantasy. A dream is the creation of our unconscious imagination, but we can shape what happens with our conscious intentions. People often ask me if, in the same way, when I live lucidly I can affect what happens in the life-dream. And my answer is yes.

I am creating my reality . . . but who am *I?*

I am the unconscious primal awareness that is conscious through Tim.

My essential nature is unconsciously dreaming the life-dream . . . but Tim can consciously shape it.

When I dream at night, my imagination creates a dreamworld from the totality of my previous experience, including my thoughts and feelings. Something comparable is happening right now. The primal imagination is unconsciously dreaming up this moment from the totality of all that has gone before. This includes Tim's private thoughts and intentions, so they can affect the way the life-dream unfolds.

Intention-Seeds

When I consciously intend something to happen in my life, it's as if I'm planting a seed in the depths of the unconscious primal awareness, where I hope it will gestate and grow so that it manifests in the life-dream.

I've often heard it said that within the seed of a tree is a whole forest. One seed will grow into a tree . . . whose seeds will grow into trees . . . whose seeds will grow into trees. It's a marvelous thought, but it's not true. There are no trees inside a seed, and recognizing this can help us understand the power and the limitations of intention.

What exists inside a seed is the genetic information necessary to turn the nutrients of the earth and the energy of the sun into a tree. The success of this will depend on both the seed and the environment. It seems to me that it's the same with the success of my intentions. Whether they become a reality depends on whether the state of the world is conducive to them flourishing. The growth of my intention-seed depends on how "realistic" it is, which is why manifesting a parking place is a lot easier than manifesting world peace!

In my experience, the most important part of the environment where my intention-seeds have to grow is my personal self—so for my intentions to manifest, I usually need to change myself first. I found this when I was a penniless musician, for example. I consciously intended to solve my money problems, but money only started flowing in my direction when I changed my ideas about money. That's because for most of my life, I'd viewed money very negatively. My life changed when I changed my story.

This is how it works for me. . . .

I immerse myself in the mystery of the moment until I'm deep awake.

I clearly frame an intention and plant it like a seed in the unconscious depths of my deeper nature.

Then I need to nourish the seed by acting to create an environment in which it can flourish.

Most important, this means transforming Tim. And as the seed gestates, my life experience begins to show me how I need to change for my intention to manifest.

If I'm unable to make the necessary changes, the seed won't grow. If I do make these changes, it often does . . . although there are inevitably factors outside of my control that may prevent this.

It's important to understand this process because there's much talk these days about how we "create our own reality," and sometimes there's the impression that, if we could simply *believe* with enough fervor, we could create the perfect life. But it's impossible for all of our intention-seeds to flourish. And believing that it's possible leads to a permanent feeling of inadequacy because we believe that we're failing to believe enough.

The truth is, sometimes the magic works and sometimes it doesn't. And sometimes it almost works. In my 20s I was very enamored with the music of Van Morrison and framed the intention that we would get the chance to meet. And . . . what do you know? Van actually called to visit someone who was living with me in the manor house I was renting . . . but, unfortunately, I was on holiday in Cuba!

Be Careful What You Wish For

My daughter, Aya Sophia, is almost eight and she loves talking philosophy. We named her Sophia after the Goddess of Wisdom, so I adore the fact that she is so eager to discuss big questions. Today we've been talking about the importance of love, and she's been saying such interesting things that I've written some of them down. Then, unexpectedly, using language I didn't know she could command, she tells me:

> "Imagination and reality sync together to make one thing. A thought transfers itself to reality. If you transfer your thought from your head to your heart, it comes out as reality . . . *but never quite as you expect*."

Her last proviso makes me laugh, because she's right: even when the magic actually works, the outcome is not always what we expect.

The ancient Romans called our deeper being the "genius." This gave rise to fairy tales about a genie in a bottle, which represents the genius trapped in the body. When we awaken the genie, he will grant our wishes. But we need to be careful what we wish for, since if we wish for the wrong thing, there will be unintended side effects . . . ask King Midas.

My friend Sean Reynolds was convinced that if he used the power of positive thought, he could become a millionaire by the time he was 40.

We were both penniless musicians in our 30s at the time, so it seemed unlikely. But he started by fixing up old houses, and within a few years he was the wealthy director of a property company.

The thing is this: He was extremely generous with his money, making other people happy—but he himself didn't seem as happy as he used to be. He'd manifested his intentions, but it didn't bring him contentment. This is why it seems so important that first and foremost, we use the magical power of intention to wake ourselves up to oneness and big love, for this is where our true satisfaction lies.

Memory and Possibility

I've just finished watching an old video of the documentary film that inspired me to take the Kogi Mamas' warning to the world nearly two decades ago. I wanted Beau to see this film because it was so important to me during a magical period in my life.

At the time, I really had no idea how I'd managed to "manifest" a 24-track recording studio from nowhere. But watching this film again, I hear what the Kogi were saying with older ears. And I realize that they wouldn't have been at all puzzled by what happened.

The Mamas say that everything comes into being in "Aluna." This is their name for what I call the primal awareness. They describe Aluna as "memory and possibility." Aluna is all that has happened and all that could happen.

When I made conscious my intention to take the Mamas' message to the world, this possibility communed in Aluna with the memory of all that had gone before. And from this meeting of memory and possibility, the future arose. The life-dream could accommodate my vision, so it materialized.

And this leaves me conscious of the intentions that are motivating me to write this book. My greatest aspiration is that it will help us wake up to oneness and big love so that we can envision together a deep awake world. Is there room in reality for that possibility, I wonder?

CHAPTER 12

THE ADVENTURE OF AWAKENING

My palms feel sweaty with fear. This time there's no escape. I've tried to get out of this crazy war by deserting from the Army and finding sanctuary here in this little shack in the woods. But it seems that I've been discovered, for I can see armed men progressing steadily toward my hideout . . . and I know how they treat deserters.

Perhaps I can run? I step gingerly outside, but I can't believe my misfortune. There are enemy soldiers moving toward me on the other side of the shack. I'm surrounded. Ripples of despair flood through me. This is the end.

Then something amazing happens . . . time freezes. No one is moving. It's like a still-life tableau. This is so strange, but it's giving me the opportunity to think about what to do. All of a sudden, I'm overwhelmed by sweet relief because I know how to get out of this alive. I've remembered something that I'm astonished I could have forgotten . . . I can fly!

As the scene bursts back into life, the soldiers rush toward me, yet I rise effortlessly into the air. They stop and stare in dumbstruck amazement. I smile down and wave a cheeky good-bye, before soaring off into the freedom of the sky . . . and then I wake up in bed laughing.

Remembering You Can Fly

I've often had war dreams in which I'm trying to escape from the conflict, and I've often had flying dreams, which are my favorite dream experience. I wanted to tell you about this particular dream, which incorporated both, because it's a great representation of what happens in my life. When I feel cornered and lost, I remember I can fly . . . metaphorically, anyway. I still haven't mastered levitation, although that would be cool.

When I'm engrossed in my story, sooner or later I remember that I can wake up. And it's always a shock that I could have forgotten. But once I remember, I become conscious of the moment. It's as if time freezes, and I step out into the timeless mystery. And my situation is transformed from a nightmare into a thrilling adventure.

I've been fascinated by flying dreams for years because I enjoy them so much. I've found that many people experience them, but what intrigues me is that everyone seems to have a different way of taking off. I just will myself to fly, and up I go. Some flap their arms. Others need to take a running jump. Some take off explosively like a rocket. Others have to launch themselves from a high building.

It seems to me that this is also true of waking up. Everyone has their own way of doing it. Some people meditate. Others dance. Some withdraw to find peace. Others throw themselves into service in the world. Everyone has their own "happy thought" that, like Peter Pan, allows them to fly.

In this book we've explored a number of wake-up techniques that I find extremely powerful, which may also work for you. Let's revisit three simple techniques that I find take me into the deep awake state. These techniques can be practiced at any time, either in formal meditation or just while taking a walk or waiting for a bus:

THE MYSTERY OF THE MOMENT

Becoming conscious of the mystery of existence is an extremely simple way to step out of my conceptual story. When I'm stuck in my dramas, I remember that in reality I have no idea what is going on, as life is always so much more than I can possibly understand. Then if I dive deeply into the mystery, my state of consciousness begins to change.

THE PLEASURE OF BREATHING

Focusing on my breath, or any particular sensation, is a powerful technique that helps me step out of my story and into the mystery. When I shift my attention away from my thoughts, my mind begins to quiet down. This makes it much easier to disengage myself from my story and become conscious of the moment.

BEING CONSCIOUS OF BEING CONSCIOUS

If I focus my attention on my subjective nature as the "I" who is witnessing all that I'm experiencing right now, I begin to become conscious that my essential nature is a spacious presence witnessing a flow of ever-changing appearances, in which all is one.

During my journey of awakening, these techniques have been my primary practices. However, I've also experimented with many other ways of becoming more conscious, such as practicing Tai Chi Chuan and yoga, exploring psychological- and personal-growth techniques, performing devotional rites and magical rituals, ingesting shamanic power-plants and psychedelic drugs, seeking out ways to be of selfless service, and so on.

Engaging with life as an adventure of awakening requires us to become passionate explorers of the mystery of life . . . and there are no limits to the ways in which we can go about this. Anything that takes us out of our habitual mind can wake us up. This includes traveling to a foreign country, reading a good book, or taking on a new challenge—because when we experience something we've never experienced before, it's much easier to appreciate the mystery of the moment.

Liberation and Bondage

I'm looking out of the vast window in my hotel suite in Las Vegas at the dazzling array of huge hotels and massive billboards glistening in the night, and it's making me wonder if my energy-saving light-bulbs at home are really doing any good! This extravagant city in the middle of the desert is outrageous, and I love it. But I can't help wondering if it's a testimony to human ingenuity or foolishness. Perhaps it's both?

I'm here with my wife, Debbie, to speak at a huge conference called "I Can Do It!" run by my publisher, Hay House. After listening to Wayne Dyer give the first major talk of the event, we've rushed up to our room to change, since we're meeting a friend named Vicki who has offered to take us out for a special evening.

I've only met Vicki once before, at a seminar in Dallas some years ago. She appeared to be an unassuming woman who didn't want to bring attention to herself. But during the break, she approached me and said,

> "Tim, I'll tell you this because we'll probably never meet again. Recently I became involved with bondage, and the first time I was tied up, I went into this extraordinary state, just like you are describing. Do you think I experienced lucid living?"

I replied,

> "Well, I've heard of 'liberation *from* bondage,' but I've never come across 'liberation *through* bondage!' That really *is* a rude awakening! But why not? Anything that knocks us out of our habitual mind-set can set us free."

Vicki had been involved with many spiritual traditions and psychological movements and was now exploring the power of the strange world of sexuality, which for many is a dark place they prefer not to visit. I love people who are willing to go to the edge in their adventure of awakening, for it's when we're brave enough to step out of comfortable social norms that we start to become truly conscious individuals.

After the seminar in Dallas, I received some wonderful e-mails signed "Vicki the Rope Slut." One read:

"The whole bondage thing is going along interestingly. I'm having a wonderful time learning and experiencing more. And as I'm doing that, I'm finding that it's easier and easier to enter the states you discussed with us. It's an interesting phenomenon.

"People get involved with bondage for different reasons: I see it as another vehicle for receiving and transmitting spiritual energy. I've had two intense bursts of 'spiritual awareness' that were life changing for me. Once was with my teacher, Swami Chetananda, and the other was at the end of a whip wielded by 'Master Skip Chasey' in a demonstration called Thunder Kiss."

Another of Vicki's e-mails read:

"This weekend coming up, I'm going to a day of meditation practice. Then a fisting demo with JLubeJack. Remember, Tim, it's all about polarities!

"Next time you come to Dallas, I'll take you to the Dungeon, where people 'get totally into their bodies,' as the illustrious Tim Freke says!"

It was my acceptance of this kind offer that has led to our expedition tonight. When Vicki realized that she would be in Vegas at the same time as Debbie and I would, she suggested we visit a dungeon in Las Vegas together. How could I say no?! It's so rare that my wife and I get to delve into something we've never experienced before.

When we meet Vicki, she's with her friend "Philip the Foole," who has studied a number of spiritual traditions and martial arts and now lectures on bondage. Debbie and I are a little nervous about what to expect because neither of us find bondage particularly alluring. We're just curious about the interesting things human beings get up to.

When we arrive in the dungeon, we're made to feel extremely welcome. There aren't many people here, so we're given a guided tour of the different "play areas," with their racks and cages. There are even two restrooms . . . a swanky one for the "doms" and a skanky one for the "subs." And what is making me laugh is that the music system is playing a remix of "State of Independence," which features Martin Luther King, Jr., passionately urging, "Let freedom ring" . . . and that strikes me as somewhat ironic in a bondage club.

I'm sure that not everyone here has the same "spiritual" perspective on bondage as Vicki and Philip, but they all seem extremely relaxed about sexuality and free in themselves. I enjoy hanging out with people who have dared to explore the depths of their own nature, wherever that happens to take them. There is a fearlessness in this that is very inspiring.

I'm enjoying myself because I always find that being in new environments brings me powerfully into the present moment. This is not a normal part of my story, so it is catapulting me into the mystery. And I can see that Debbie is feeling the same.

It's all too cold and clinical to feel sexy, but it's a privilege to have been welcomed into another world for a few hours. And I'm thinking about how much fun it will be to talk about this experience tomorrow, during my presentation at the I Can Do It! conference.

We're ready to go now—I don't want to be up so late that I'm not fresh for my presentation. The owner is apologetic that there have been so few people here because it would normally be steaming on a Friday night. He explains that it's the birthday of one of the members, and a group has gotten together at a local bar for an evening of karaoke before heading back to the dungeon afterward. Now I'm shocked. Karaoke! That's taking voluntary humiliation too far!

Living on the Edge

I often talk about Vicki and her experiences at my seminars, since it really detonates any superficial preconceptions about what waking up entails. It's a way of pushing people to see the total freedom that arises when we live lucidly and step out of our social conditioning.

I mentioned Vicki at a seminar in the U.K. recently because I wanted to shock the group awake. This time, however, the joke was on me. A glamorous lady "of a certain age" promptly informed me that she had her bondage gear in the back of her car, and she was going on after the seminar to "have a scene" . . . with the local vicar. God, I love it when people feel free to be themselves!

We don't have to get involved in bondage, of course, to transform our lives into an adventure of awakening. But I do feel that we have to acknowledge how free we truly are, and this can lead us to act in ways that others who are confined by narrow social norms find difficult to understand.

I abandoned any conventional ideas about what we should and shouldn't do years ago. Now I simply follow the natural morality of love. It seems to me that if we act from love, making sure that no one gets hurt, we're free to do whatever we want. (Although in Vicki's case, a certain amount of getting hurt is voluntarily welcomed.)

The ethical rules that confine most people are society's attempt to give us guidelines about how to live together harmoniously. If we're lost in separateness, we go along with the social norms to fit in and avoid retribution. But true morality is not about rules. It's about our state of consciousness. If we're awake and experiencing big love, we don't need rules to stop us from taking advantage of others, since we can't help but act lovingly.

In the Christian Gnostic tradition, which I've written about in many books, the deep awake state is called "gnosis" or "knowledge" because it's the state of true self-knowledge. And there's a line in the Gospel of Philip that explains:

"Those who are free because of gnosis become slaves because of love."

This puts it beautifully. When we wake up, we are liberated from our limiting conditioning and free to live in any way we choose. Yet the oneness we experience means that we become slaves to love. I don't think this passage is meant to have any "bondage" overtones . . .

but you never know. Some of those Gnostics were pretty out-there libertines.

Embodied Enlivenment

Exploring sexuality and sensuality is a powerful and enjoyable way to wake up. When we make love, we can commune physically, emotionally, and spiritually. Most of the time we hide behind the masks of our social personas and cover our bodies with clothes. But when we meet sexually, we have the opportunity to be naked with each other, both literally and metaphorically. And when we connect as one in love, expressing animal passions—which might otherwise be ugly— becomes a liberating and enlivening experience.

Not long ago, I was invited to work with a group of Tantric teachers known as "the Divine Feminine Institute," who help people explore sexuality and sensuality as a way of waking up. They adopt a much softer approach than Vicki, which fits more with my particular nature. I immediately fell in love with these wonderfully awake people because they were so present in their bodies and affectionately tactile. And my philosophy harmonized beautifully with their Tantric practices because for me, the awakening of the body is an important aspect of living lucidly in the world.

I've found that practicing physical disciplines, such as Tai Chi Chuan and yoga, can be a great way to embody the deep awake state. But I've also found that ecstatic dancing can work just as well. Anything that relaxes and opens the body can also relax and open the mind, which makes it easier to enter deeply into the mystery of the moment.

Lucid living is embodied enlivenment. It is a state of consciousness that reaches right down into our physical nature and changes how we engage with the sensual world. We find ourselves delighting in the pleasures of existence because we are conscious enough to really relish them. This is why in the Hindu tradition, people in the deep awake state are sometimes called *bhogis* or "super enjoyers."

The Indian teacher Osho suggested that the ideal figure to

represent "a new order of humanity" would be "Zorba the Buddha." This is because such a person would combine the spiritual equanimity of the Buddha with the passion of Zorba the Greek, who enjoyed life to the max. Osho is a controversial figure with whom I've never studied, so I have no opinions about the man himself. But I do know that this is a wonderful image for the 21st-century spiritual ideal of being both enlightened and enlivened.

Updating the Operating System

Before being able to write the end of this chapter, I've had to attend to some technical problems with my computer. It kept crashing on me, so I've installed a new operating system, and now things are running much better. I'm telling you this because it works for me as an analogy for an important aspect of the journey of awakening.

So far I've been talking about how we need to keep boldly experimenting with ways to free ourselves from our habitual states. But there is another, complementary aspect of the process of awakening that I also want to address. And that is the need to consciously change those habits of thought that prevent us from living lucidly.

Our habitual ways of thinking are like an internal "operating system" that governs how we respond to what happens to us. If we want to keep growing, we need to constantly update our operating system; otherwise, it starts crashing on us, and we lose our capacity to feel enlivened.

To become deep awake, we need to enter the mystery of the moment, but we're unable to remain in this state if we're unconsciously pulled back into our story by certain habits of thought. So we need to become conscious of those thought patterns that cause us problems, and replace them with new ones that help us wake up.

There's nothing wrong with habits per se. We need habits. Learning is a process of developing habitual ways of dealing with situations. The whole of nature could be seen as one big habit. Over the billions of years since the big bang, nature has gotten in the habit of things being the way they are. But through the process of evolution, nature gradually develops new and more interesting habits.

We are a part of nature and need to keep evolving. We can do this by retaining those habits of thought that are working for us and changing those that are not. And this requires us to become conscious of how we're thinking. The difference between an unconscious habit and a conscious habit is that the latter is *chosen*. We follow an unconscious habit of thought because we can't resist it. We follow a conscious habit of thought willingly.

The problem is that our habits of thought have a psychological gravity that pulls our attention toward them, unless we're conscious enough to resist. Many of our habitual thoughts are common in our culture, and these are even harder to resist because they have the weight of the collective adding to their gravitational pull. We all have different negative patterns of thought, but here are some of the common ones that many of us wrestle with:

I'm not good enough.

The world is cruel and uncaring.

I wish I hadn't done that in the past.

I'm anxious about the future.

If we become consumed by such thoughts, it's impossible to feel enlivened—so we need to question whether they offer us the best way of looking at our situation, and to consider if there's a better response to the challenges we face. Then we can update our operating system so that we adopt a wiser approach.

This doesn't mean denying our faults . . . or that the world can be cruel . . . or that we've made mistakes . . . or that the future can be frightening. It means *also* recognizing that our essential nature is all goodness . . . that the world is replete with love . . . that we can learn from our past errors . . . and that we can shape the future if we become more conscious. If we integrate these thoughts into our internal operating system, it becomes much easier to live lucidly.

Seriously destructive habits of thought are sometimes called "neuroses." We tend to think of our neuroses as rooted in the past because they usually arise from some faulty piece of learning when we were younger. But this can be a disempowering way of looking at things, as we can't change the past. I prefer to focus on how we re-create our neuroses in the present moment. Every time we unconsciously go along with a neurotic pattern of thought, we rewrite it on our internal hard drive. But every time we become conscious of it, we have the opportunity to overwrite it with a new way of thinking.

Sometimes habits of thought are so ingrained that we have to become conscious of them over and over again before they change. Sometimes a superficial habit won't change until we unearth its roots in a deeper habit. But all of this can only ever happen in the present moment. Now is the opportunity to change.

My Habitual Defenses

Debbie is being really pigheaded, and it's getting annoying. She's just refusing to see my point of view, when I've explained it a million times. She's wrong about this and she knows it. But she's in a grumpy mood and doesn't want to lose the argument.

Oh shit! I've just called her "Caroline" . . . my ex-wife's name. What does that mean? I know exactly what it means, but I don't want to admit it. I'm projecting my past all over the present. I'm not arguing with Debbie. I'm lost in myself.

I feel attacked and I'm putting up my habitual defenses. I'm doing what I always do. I'm cleverly twisting the conversation to make myself right. That's what my dad does . . . this is all conditioning.

I want to stop arguing, but the bad words keeping coming out of my mouth. It's like I'm running on automatic. I want to let go, but my story is so sticky. I need to be deep awake and deal with this creatively, but I'm lost in judgment . . . anger . . . fear . . . selfishness.

But now Debbie isn't saying anything. In fact, she's smiling at me sheepishly. Oh my God, she's just dropped the whole thing. And that's taken away all the energy from our quarrel. I feel like I'm waking up from a silly dream. I feel really stupid . . . in a good way.

We're suddenly in the mystery of the moment together. She looks radiantly beautiful. My habitual defenses have come down. I'm present and open. I feel loved and loving. I'm soft and vulnerable. Being in love is being vulnerable.

After we've made up, I need to take some time to really be conscious of what has just happened. I responded like an automaton from my habitual mind, and the result was an unnecessary conflict. I want to clearly see those patterns I keep playing out.

I don't need to give myself a hard time about it, since these patterns are just the result of my conditioning. But I do need to recognize my habits of mind and consciously choose to change them so that next time a similar situation arises, I can be the one to step out of the drama into the mystery, and set us both free.

Transcend and Transform

The process of awakening has two complementary aspects—which shouldn't be a surprise, as everything is predicated on the polarity paradox. We need to do all we can to become more conscious, *and* we need to change those habits of mind that keep us asleep in separateness. We need to *transcend* our separate identity so we wake up to our essential nature, and we need to *transform* our separate identity so we can stay awake and live lucidly.

When we truly understand that the most important factor that governs how much we enjoy life is how conscious we are, waking up ceases to be something we pay attention to occasionally. Instead, our everyday existence is transformed into an adventure of awakening, in which we're always seeking out experiences that will make us more conscious.

But it soon becomes obvious that staying awake is a real challenge, since our habitual thought patterns constantly pull us back to the story of separateness. This means that we need to clearly recognize our habits of mind. Then we can replace old ways of thinking that keep us asleep in separateness with new ways of thinking that help us live lucidly.

The way we think governs what we experience, which is why spiritual philosophy can help wake us up. However, I've found that some "spiritual" teachings have just the opposite effect. So I now want to challenge some common spiritual ideas that can prevent people from awakening.

I'm going to explore how much of popular spirituality is bogged down in either/or thinking, which traps us in separateness. Then I'm going to show how spiritual misunderstandings cause us to regress rather than evolve. But first I want to question the pernicious idea that we have an enemy within whom we need to defeat if we want to wake up . . . because war really sucks . . . especially when it's inside your own head.

CHAPTER 13

THE ENEMY WITHIN?

Things have been sticky lately. Sometimes life's like that. I keep getting lost in my dramas. I wake up for a little and then I'm sucked in again. So I'm allowing myself a day off from family responsibilities and the demands of work to give myself the opportunity to do some in-depth meditation, as well as some yoga and Tai Chi Chuan. And hopefully this will sort me out.

Everyone I know goes through rough patches and then comes out the other side. It's as if we're all on our own personal journey, with its own ever-changing terrain. Sometimes I feel like I'm skipping through a meadow, while a friend is staggering through a desert. But at the end of my meadow is a quagmire I must now slowly traverse, while my friend is relaxing at an oasis.

Life is a process of becoming more conscious than we presently are, so we're all on an expedition into uncharted territory. Sometimes the going is easy, and sometimes the going gets tough. Yet I still harbor the fantasy that it should be possible for things to always be easy . . . although I have no good reason to believe this.

Every challenge I face gives way to a new challenge. Just the fact that I'm aging all the time means that I'm constantly confronted with new dilemmas. This requires me to constantly become conscious about things I've previously been unconscious about. And this means that I inevitably go in and out of being more conscious.

We're all in transit. I used to imagine that there were people somewhere, probably in a cave up in the Himalayas, who had arrived at some perfect state. But having hung out in spiritual circles for so long, I've given up this idea. Sooner or later you hear the dirt on everyone, and it turns out that we're all the same. We all have to climb mountains, and we all sometimes lose our footing.

Realizing this has helped me let go of the unrealistic expectation that Tim could be perfect. I understand that to be human is to be partly conscious and partly unconscious, so I can always become more conscious. And this has made me more accepting of Tim's limitations and foibles.

But I still find it hard to break the habit of being horribly critical of myself when life gets sticky, as it has been recently. I guess this is to be expected. When I'm lost in my story, I temporarily forget a lot of the wisdom I've learned. I regress to a less conscious state where I repeat the same old patterns and get lost in the same old thoughts.

Sometimes I project my problems onto others and blame them for my states. Even if I'm conscious enough to avoid doing that, I'm still left with Tim and his inadequacies . . . so I blame him. But over the years, I've seen that this just makes matters worse. My self-loathing keeps me embroiled in my story. The solution is not to fight myself, but to love myself. Love is the answer . . . and this is no exception.

From what I gather from other people, I'm not alone in finding it difficult to love myself. This is a challenge we all must engage on our journey of awakening. Yet when it comes to loving ourselves, I find some of the traditional teachings of spirituality particularly *un*helpful. Indeed, I'd go so far as to say that in my life, they've been a large part of the problem.

Spiritual teachings often tell us that there is an enemy within who leads us astray, so we need to enter into a purifying civil war of the soul. There's a lower self we must subdue in gladiatorial combat. There is an ego we need to destroy, but it is determined not to submit. It's a relentless campaign against a wily opponent who will stop at nothing to hold us prisoner.

Yet I have found that waging a war against myself doesn't wake me up to oneness but merely fragments me further. I now think that there are two Tims . . . the bad Tim, who is causing all of my troubles; and the good Tim, who is busy judging the bad Tim.

The problem seems to be that good Tim is too weak to triumph over bad Tim. But actually the problem is the war itself. Peace is only possible when I stop identifying with either of these Tims and instead become conscious of my deeper identity as the "I" of awareness, which is witnessing the whole silly drama, so I can embrace all of Tim with big love.

Yet here I am in the middle of this rough patch, and I've been doing what I usually do in such situations . . . I've been taking sides. I've been trying to work out strategies for good Tim to triumph over bad Tim. But that's just a symptom of things being sticky; it's not going to resolve the conflict. The only solution is to let go of my internal bickering and sink into the mystery of the moment so that I'm conscious enough to love myself, forgive myself, and not take myself so damn seriously.

Gracie's idea ... we're addicted to emotional attachments (of being right, proving another wrong, victim mentality)

The Traitorous Ego

I've been invited to talk to a group of people who are on a spiritual retreat in a magnificent old country house. They're a sincere bunch of seekers whose guru died sometime ago. I've been chatting with them during the breaks, and everyone is conscious and kind in a natural way.

But the funny thing is that whenever they start talking about "spirituality," everything gets complicated and theoretical. And then our interaction starts to feel inauthentic. It's as if their "spiritual" ideas are standing in the way of them really understanding the simple message at the heart of spirituality.

I often find that the simplicity of what I have to say is more easily appreciated by newbies to the waking-up business than by those who are seasoned spiritual travelers. This is because newbies display an openness that Zen master Shunryu Suzuki calls "beginner's mind," while the spiritually experienced can be so caught up in their preconceptions that they find it hard to see the obvious, which is what waking up is really all about.

Right now, for example, I'm enjoying a conversation with an earnest young man who has read a lot of books on mysticism, and he's clearly struggling under the weight of all the spiritual theories he's accumulated. The question he wants answered next is a common one:

"How the hell can I get rid of my ego?!"

"Well, first tell me what you mean by the word 'ego,' because it's used in so many different ways."

"I'm not sure . . . I guess it's what you call the separate self."

"In which case, it seems to me that it would be disastrous to get rid of your ego. You need an ego to function in the life-dream. I don't tell my kids to get rid of their egos. I help them develop healthy, self-confident egos so that they have a strong sense of their individuality, along with the ability to put necessary boundaries between themselves and others. The idea that we've spent our childhood building up an ego we now need to destroy seems perverse."

"But when I'm caught up with my ego, I get self-centered and arrogant."

"Look . . . having an 'ego' is as much a natural part of being human as having a heart. But you don't want to be lost in the ego, as this leads to all sorts of suffering. You need to be conscious of *both* your ego *and* your essential nature as the oneness of awareness. You need to transcend and include your ego within your deeper identity. The ego doesn't need fighting. It needs loving."

"But my ego is unlovable. It's like I've got a crazy person in my head who won't shut up."

"I know what you mean. I'm all too familiar with the crazy ramblings of my mind when it's become agitated because it's finding it hard to process something that's happening in my life."

"Well, maybe that's my question . . . how do I shut up my crazy mind?"

"Spiritual traditions that encourage some sort of inner conflict often make the mind an enemy, but it really isn't. The mind is a great blessing, not an adversary to be silenced. Our ability to think is what makes us human. If we didn't think, we wouldn't be wise, we'd be stupid. You have a fine mind, and I'm really enjoying engaging with it in this conversation."

"That's nice of you to say. But believe me, from the inside, my mind is like some malicious traitor who's hiding out in my own head, always distracting me from my spiritual goals with wayward thoughts."

"Like everything in duality, the mind has a positive aspect and a negative aspect. It helps and it hinders. The problems you're talking about arise when we're only conscious of the mind and not of our deeper identity as well. Then the mind runs in its familiar neurotic grooves. But as soon as we become more conscious, the mind starts to calm down and we're able to see things in new ways."

"But why is the mind so agitated in the first place?"

"The mind's job is to think, like the heart's job is to beat. It's constantly trying to piece together a coherent conceptual story to help us live well and stay safe. But sometimes it just doesn't have the information it needs to make sense of things. It can't find solutions to the challenges we face, so it gets caught up in repetitive cycles of anxious thoughts."

"That's what I find so disturbing."

"But even this isn't *just* a bad thing. Psychological suffering tells us that there's something wrong with the way we are thinking, just as physical suffering tells us there's something wrong with our body."

"So how do you find out what's wrong and put things right?"

"You need to step out of your mind into the mystery of the moment. Your thoughts won't stop, but they will fade into your peripheral awareness. Witness your thoughts coming and going, rather than being engrossed in them. Then you'll start to become deep awake. And the mind will react to this new state of consciousness by thinking in new ways."

"So you're saying that the solution isn't to get rid of the mind, but to focus my attention elsewhere."

"Exactly. There only appears to be an enemy within when we're lost in the either/or duality of separateness. When we live lucidly, everything finds its place."

"That's an attractive idea, but the reality is that I often experience something inside that actively wants to prevent me from waking up. For instance, I've recently been going much deeper into meditation, and I've begun to feel as if my separateness is dissolving into the oneness of things. But there's a little voice of fear that stops me from letting go into the void. I see it as my ego, which needs to die if I am to become enlightened, and it won't go without a fight. I want to overcome it, but I can't."

"I've experienced the same thing many times during my journey of awakening, and I also used to see it as the pernicious voice of my ego seducing me back to a state of ignorance. But these days, I see this voice as an expression of my innate wisdom."

"Wisdom? What do you mean by that?!"

"We become conscious through separateness. Our separate identity as individuals in the world is the foundation from which we can wake up to our essential identity as the oneness of awareness. Once we have a strong sense of our separate identity, we can successfully transcend it without floating off into limitless emptiness and losing our grounding in the world. If we go too deep prematurely, we can lose our sense of separateness, and this is not healthy at all. It can lead to a disconnection from life and from others. We can become ineffective, spaced-out, and even 'insane' because we've lost our grounding in the world."

"So the voice that stops me from completely dissolving into the void is keeping me safely anchored in the world of separateness."

"Exactly. If you believe that you need to 'kill your ego,' then that wise voice will of course appear to be an internal enemy sabotaging your awakening. However, once you realize that you need to be conscious of *both* your separate identity *and* your essential identity . . . not either/or . . . you start to see that what you took to be an enemy is actually a friend, who is making sure that you make the journey of awakening at the right pace."

"I've come across lots of spiritual teachers who have told me that I need to overcome my ego or my mind . . . and now you're telling me that's a mistake."

"Yes. And I'd be wary of teachers who encourage internal conflict, since some of them are dangerous. They may claim to be in the business of waking people up, but actually they want to suck people into their little spiritual cult. And a common way of keeping people in a cult is to encourage them to fight an unwinnable war with themselves. This means that they never really get anywhere, so they always come back for more teachings. And it also means that when people finally get around to asking difficult questions that could lead them out of the cult, they're told that this is just their crazy mind speaking . . . or their ego acting out and resisting the words of the master."

"Maybe all of my questions to you are just my ego resisting the words of the master?"

"Or maybe you're actually a really smart guy with a good mind and a healthy ego, who thinks for himself and dares to doubt? That's the way it looks to me."

Major Achievement and Private Pleasures

For me, waking up isn't about winning the battle between good Tim and bad Tim. It's about seeing that there really is no "Tim" at all. When I witness Tim from the deep awake state, what I see is a complex of concepts and memories that give rise to hopes and fears, habitual ways of thinking and reacting, patterns of speech and behavior. "Tim" is made up of body parts and psychological characteristics. What gives me the unshakable sense of being an individual is not Tim. It is the "I" of my deeper nature. The "I" is the one that binds the fragments of Tim into the semblance of a someone.

Tim is not even a unified persona that integrates all of my concepts and memories into a consistent whole. Rather, Tim consists of many personas that surface at different times in response to different situations. The word "persona" means "mask," and it seems to me that I wear a whole selection of different masks to meet the world. There are lots of Tims with different stories and competing agendas.

So in one way there's no Tim, and in another way there are many Tims, some of whom really don't get along with each other. I've even given them playful names. There's Mr. Mystic, who takes the business of waking up very intensely and thinks that everything else is a big

Conflicting personas vs. transpersonal identity

waste of time. He doesn't get along at all with Mr. Rock 'n' Roll, who's into self-expression and a bit of a hedonist. He wants Mr. Mystic to loosen up because he can't see the attraction of spiritual discipline.

There have been times in my life where one or the other of these personas has set themselves up as CEO of Tim, Inc. But the other persona has always managed to engineer a boardroom coup, which has completely changed the way Tim does business. Actually, of course, I need to both wake up to oneness and express my individual nature. There are times to be both self-indulgent and self-disciplined. But try telling that to Mr. Mystic and Mr. Rock 'n' Roll!

There's also Major Achievement. Every so often the Major strides into my consciousness to remind me that I ought to be doing something significant with my life. Tim has been a big disappointment and is letting him down. He needs to buck up his ideas, or he'll never amount to anything. Major Achievement often gets in arguments with Private Pleasures, who is content to be a simple guy who enjoys the everyday delights of life.

Whenever I identify with one of my personas, I set up an internal struggle with my other personas. There's temporary relief when one becomes dominant, but the others don't go away. They bide their time and launch a counteroffensive, which leaves me confused and battered.

But none of these conflicting personas is my true identity. They are all impostors. And when I identify with one of my fragmentary personas, I alienate myself from the other fragments of myself. Only when I wake up to my deeper transpersonal identity—and hold them all within a loving embrace—can I start to initiate peace talks in which all parties' points of view are acknowledged and respected.

I don't need to reject some part of myself to wake up. I need to embrace all that I am. I need to be conscious of my spacious, all-embracing, impersonal essence, which transcends and includes all of my warring personas. Then I can start to integrate all of the aspects of "Tim" into a coherent whole.

Consciousness and Energy

I've just come home after a great seminar and I'm feeling intensely enlivened. People often ask me how I manage to expend so much energy when I run these events. The answer is that when I explore philosophy, I become intently focused on the deep awake state, which makes me extremely energized. And that's because I am consciously entering the deep sleep state, which is the primal life force I merge with to recharge at night.

But now that the seminar is over, I'm becoming tired. I'm going to put my feet up and relax for the evening. In fact I think I'll allow myself to become comfortably semiconscious watching TV. Soon I'll need to go unconscious altogether. But in the morning I'll be revitalized with the energy to explore consciousness again.

I used to have the crazy idea that I should permanently inhabit an ultraconscious state. When I failed to do so, I regarded it as a spiritual failure because I imagined that I was being seduced into unconsciousness by my perfidious ego. But I don't see things like that anymore. And this feels good, for it has liberated me from chasing an unattainable ideal. Now I allow myself to flow between different states of consciousness. I've stopped fighting the natural process of life.

Consciousness requires energy, which is why when the energy runs out, we go unconscious. Sometimes I have the energy to be ultraconscious and deep awake. Sometimes I become so tired that I have to go deep asleep. Sometimes I can manage to be in the waking state but not the deep awake state. This is all part of the natural way of things.

At my seminars, I'm often asked if I'm permanently deep awake. This makes me laugh because these days, the idea of anything in my experience being permanent seems ridiculous. States of consciousness come and go. That's the way it is for all of us.

I remember when I was in Mumbai asking Ramesh if he was always conscious of oneness, and he replied . . . "Whenever I think about it." At the time I didn't know what he meant. Now I realize he was telling me that the oneness was obvious whenever he placed his attention on it. But the focus of his attention wasn't always there. How could it be? This fits with my own experience, since I find that the deep awake state is available to me whenever I focus my attention on my essential nature. But sometimes I don't have the energy to do this and that's okay. Sometimes I need to rest.

Consciousness comes and goes. When I used to fight my unconsciousness, it turned the adventure of awakening into a perpetual struggle. I've come to accept that sometimes I'm very awake and sometimes I'm not. Even getting lost in the story of Tim is okay because this is the way I experience things that will ultimately make me more conscious. In my experience, I just need to be authentic with whatever is happening for me. There's no need to fight the flow of my life.

There's a time for everything under heaven. It's getting bogged down anywhere for too long that I try to avoid. When my attention isn't fixed, I can go with the flow. Then it's all okay. And right now that means that vegging out in front of the TV is okay. And I'm going to enjoy doing just that for an hour or so . . . and then I'm off to bed to dissolve into the void.

○ ○ ○

CHAPTER 14

BOTH/AND THINKING

I've been enjoying a late-night session of philosophy with Peter Gandy . . . and our mutual friend Jack Daniels. It's a continuation of an ongoing conversation that we started more than 30 years ago about this bizarre business we call "life," and we're still finding new answers . . . and new questions.

I met Peter shortly before I woke up for the first time when I was 12. We were both members of a troupe of young actors for whom I wrote a play called *The Wrong Way,* which was inspired by my experience on the hill. I directed it in an old church that doubled as a theater. We were just kids, so it was a big deal in our little town, attracting the television media and making a splash in the local papers.

Peter and I became philosophical sparring partners in our teens and did every mad thing we could think of to explore consciousness. Much later, our adventures bore fruit in the form of some great books we wrote together about Gnosticism. Over the years, our ideas have become so entwined that we've shaped a philosophy between us. Tonight we've been talking about the "polarity paradox" that underlies existence, and exploring the importance of "both/and" thinking on the journey of awakening.

"You know, Pete, the more I get into this both/and approach to things, the more obvious it becomes that a great deal of spirituality is actually bogged down in either/or thinking. There's always one pole of the polarity who is the bad guy who really shouldn't be there. There's something to reject . . . the ego . . . the rational mind . . . negative thinking . . . carnal pleasures . . . personal attachments . . ."

"That's crazy because it's unrealistic. You can't exile one of the poles of a polarity."

"For example, people say that if we want to be enlightened, we shouldn't have any judgments. Judgments are 'bad.' But that can't be right, since you can't live without making judgments. I mean, picture this . . . I'm walking down a dark alley at night in London and there's a guy coming toward me wearing a hood . . . but I try not to be judgmental, so I say to myself . . . it's probably Saint Francis of Assisi."

"Not a good idea. Especially if it turns out to be some punk after your wallet."

"It seems to me that I need to make judgments all the time. But I hate it when I'm stuck in my judgments, because then I can't see things from other perspectives. And I love it when I'm lucid, because then I can make judgments as I go about the necessary business of discriminating things—but I'm also conscious of my essential nature, which is utterly accepting and nonjudgmental."

"It's not either/or . . . it's both/and."

"Here's another spiritual idea I used to take seriously, but now seems ludicrous. . . . If we were truly enlightened, we'd have no fear."

"You're right; that's crazy. Fear is a necessary part of life, which is why we sometimes feel it."

"Exactly. I've tried to instill into my kids a certain amount of fear . . . of the road outside our house, for instance . . . because it will help them stay safe."

"Fear alerts us to danger."

"The way I see it, the problem isn't fear . . . it's *just* fear. When I'm lost in the story of Tim, it can get horribly scary. But when I'm lucid, I know it's all okay, really. That doesn't mean that I never feel fear, but it does mean that I'm able to deal with it."

"'Feel the fear and do it anyway' . . ."

"I was going to give up smoking before I came across that book."

"How about this one . . . to be enlightened, we need to become completely selfless. Did you upload that crazy cookie?"

"Of course . . . and I constantly felt bad about how selfish I was."

"Well, as an old mate, I have to tell you that sometimes that was justified."

"True enough."

"But I also want to reassure you that it really is okay to be selfish as well as selfless. If you don't look after yourself, there would be no one to be selfless."

"Well, thank you, bro, that's a great relief."

"My stepfather told me a great story the other day. When he was working as a vicar in the Church of England, he was troubled by the bit in the New Testament where Jesus tells his disciples to give everything to the poor. He kept thinking . . . it sounds lovely, but if I did that I'd just become one of the poor myself. And where's the sense in that?"

"The funny thing is that when I'm lucid, I find that being self-less is the most selfishly enjoyable state I know. It's like the two become one."

"Yes . . . but when push comes to shove, you're still ready to put Tim and his family first. I mean . . . you're not inviting homeless people to come and live in your house."

"I feel like I'm constantly trying to find the right relationship between my selfish needs and my selfless love."

"That's how it is to live with the paradox that we're both separate and all one at the same time."

"It seems silly now, but when I was younger I really used to believe that if I could only be spiritual enough, I'd become some sort of totally selfless, nonjudgmental, fearless, über-being! A Great Soul who was completely perfect."

"I seem to remember that half the time you thought you already were perfect . . . I know I did."

"You're right. I veered dramatically from being convinced that I was some sort of enlightened genius and thinking that I was a complete asshole."

"That sounds familiar."

"But now I've come to terms with the fact that I'm both."

"Not a complete genius, but a partial genius. Not a complete asshole, but a partial asshole."

"When I was speaking in Maui recently, an interesting guy there asked me to guess what organ of the body develops first in the human fetus . . . do you know?"

"The heart maybe?"

"The asshole. We all start as assholes, and we all stay assholes till the day we die . . . but not just assholes."

"We're Great Souls and assholes."

"That's an undeniable case of both/and."

Traveling and Arriving

I've been reading this article in a spiritual magazine on "being present" that I'd like to discuss with you. It's counseling us to stop thinking about the past and the future and instead pay attention to the now. This is a very popular idea these days. And that's great, as anything that brings us into the mystery of the moment is all right with me. That's the secret of enlivenment.

But there's something wrong about this article, which troubles me. It means well, but it's full of either/or thinking. It offers a choice between *either* being present *or* being lost in time. But in my experience, it's not either/or . . . it's both/and.

The idea of just being present sounds wise, but it's actually bonkers. If I stopped remembering yesterday and planning for the future, I wouldn't know where I'd come from or where I was going. I'd be lost, not enlightened. As a parent, my job is to convince my children that they need to stop just being concerned about the now and start to become conscious of the consequences of their actions in the future. Just being in the now would be a regression to childhood.

It's true that if we want to experience the childlike bliss of simply *being,* we need to focus our attention on the mystery of the moment. But this doesn't mean we shouldn't concern ourselves with the past and future. Rather, we need to be conscious of *both* the eternal now *and* the flow of time. And it's when we're conscious of both that we live lucidly.

The Zen masters compare being awake to "collecting fruit in a bottomless basket." I love this because it captures the experience of being in the mystery of the moment. New experiences arise and pass away, without my clinging to anything. Wonderful! But, of course, if I actually collected fruit in a bottomless basket, I would end up with nothing to eat. And likewise, just being in the mystery of the moment won't enable me to meet the needs of being a person in time.

Luckily, I have the freedom to look at things in both ways at once. I can bring the mystery of the moment into my focused awareness and allow the process of time to fade into my peripheral awareness. Then, when I need to, I can bring the process of time into my focused awareness and allow the mystery of the moment to linger in my peripheral awareness.

I am conscious through my concepts, which create my story. And since all of my concepts come from the past, this means that the past and present are intrinsically bound together. I can't have one without the other, so trying to do so is futile. But that doesn't mean I have to be lost in regret or anticipation. I can also be fully present to the magnificence of the moment.

I've come to see that I'm both traveling and arriving in every moment. My life is a journey in which I'm constantly arriving at my destination, which is here and now. And I'm also traveling onward into a future that will become here and now.

I first understood this when I was at school with Peter Gandy. We'd been studying a poem by Philip Larkin called "Poetry of Departures," which was about the idea of daring to just get up and go, leaving behind your familiar life. This got us into a discussion about whether it was better to travel or arrive. And we decided that the best way to find out was to just get up and go ourselves.

So that's what we did. We collected whatever small amounts of money we could find and set off with the intention of hitchhiking to

Paris. At 17 it seemed like a bold adventure, which concerned our parents, but there was no stopping our philosophical experiment.

We caught a cheap ferry to Calais and landed in France the following evening. It was sleeting, and we trudged through the biting wind singing the Beatles' "The Long and Winding Road" because it felt suitably poignant. Eventually we got a lift to Caen, but we arrived too late for the youth hostel, so we slept on the porch.

The next day we discovered that, by some strange coincidence, the members of a big band from a school in our hometown were staying in this hostel. Stranger still, Peter used to play drums for this band, and one of the members was a certain girl that he fancied . . . so that's when we parted.

Peter went back home on the bus with the big band and the cute girl. I carried on hitching to Paris. This felt fair enough. Peter had said that it was more important to travel. It was I who'd felt that it was more important to arrive.

It was quite a trip, but eventually I found myself triumphantly standing under the Eiffel Tower, wondering how I would get back to England. And that's when I realized something that resolved the question I had set out to answer. So I bought a postcard of the tower, wrote a message to myself, and sent it home so that it would be waiting for me upon my return.

I still have this card, on which the young Tim has written . . .

Arriving is a point on a continuum of traveling.

Traveling is a process of constantly arriving.

Yuk and Yum

I'm talking on the phone with Peter, as I do most mornings, chewing the cud about life. I love Peter because he is such a paradox . . . much like myself. He's a respected classicist, but he used to be a street performer. I wanted to be a musician, but I ended up a philosopher. These days, I'm experimenting with stand-up philosophy, while he's playing with stand-up comedy. So our conversations tend to be a playful mix of insight and laughter.

Our discussion this morning has ranged from the sublime to the ridiculous. And we've also made time to enjoy moaning about our personal complaints. We've known each other for so long that we're able to be real about whatever happens to be going on. Right now Peter can tell I'm a little out of sorts, so I explain,

"I'm pissed off. It's raining, I've got a toothache, and I need a holiday."

"Well, matey, we'd all like sunshine without rain, pleasure without pain, play without work, life without death . . . but you know this isn't going to happen."

"You're right. Life is predicated on polarity, so you can't have yum without yuk."

"I'm with Empedocles, who saw life as a dance of opposites in a state of love or strife."

"I can get that. When we try to embrace one pole while exiling the other, it sets up strife between the opposites. But if we allow both poles, we can embrace things as they are."

"Well . . . if we want to embrace things as they are, we'd better come to terms with the fact that life is good and bad, kind and cruel, beautiful and ugly, funny and tragic . . ."

"Yet somewhere along the line I seem to have been sucked in by the ridiculous fantasy that it's possible to arrive at some perfect place, where I'd have good without bad, joy without suffering, clever without stupid, hope without fear . . ."

"But that day never comes and never will."

"Actually, I feel relieved to realize that. It stops me from trying to have yum without yuk, so I can start to embrace both as inevitable aspects of life."

"It's about living with polarity, not trying to exile one of the poles. When life is shitty, I try not to forget that it's also magical. And when life is fun, I try not to forget that it's also agonizing."

"That's the key to compassion—because then you're aware of the suffering of others, even when things are going well for you."

"If you want to dine out on life, you need to be able to enjoy a sweet-and-sour dish."

"So the bad news is that there's always something to complain about. But the good news is that there's always something to appreciate, too. Paranoid people focus on what's bad about life. I prefer to take a 'pronoid' approach and focus on what's good, because it feels much better that way."

"But that doesn't mean ignoring the bad. I can't stand all that positive-thinking stuff, because it's important to allow negative thoughts. Let's face it, a lot of things about life really stink. And if we want to be authentic, we need to acknowledge this."

"You're right. There's something missing from the 'it's all perfect' school of spirituality. From one perspective, of course, it *is* all perfect. But it's also decidedly not perfect from another. And if it wasn't also imperfect, things couldn't evolve."

"When we try to ignore the yucky bits of life, we can't embrace things as they actually are. And we're heading for a nasty shock when, sooner or later, there's so much yuk that we can't avoid it."

"As a confirmed pronoid, I prefer to focus on yum. But sometimes I have to make yuk my focus because it's necessary if I want things to get better."

"It's about seeing negativity more positively. Good things come from bad things. We often learn more from suffering than from contentment."

"For me, the secret is to live lucidly. When I'm conscious of my essential nature, I can embrace everything just as it is. Then I can accept that the price of pleasure is pain."

"Sounds like a bargain . . . I'm buying."

"Me, too. I'm with Rumi . . . 'the honey is worth the sting.'"

The Trickle of Honey

There is yum and yuk in every moment. So the secret to dealing with yucky situations is to remember the ways in which things are also yummy. I'd like to share with you an old Sufi teaching story that illustrates this idea. I first came across it years ago, but I still find it useful. It's a romantic tale about a young maiden trapped in a tower. The prince wants to rescue her, but he has no way of getting a rope up to the top of the tower. So he comes up with a cunning plan.

The prince asks the maiden to pour a trickle of honey down the side of the tower. Then he finds a small insect and ties on to it a thread of cotton. He places the insect at the bottom of the trickle of honey. The insect slowly eats its way up the tower to the princess, who takes the thread of cotton. To the thread the prince attaches a piece of string, which the princess pulls up to her. Then to the string the prince attaches a rope. And when the princess has pulled up the string and has the rope, she climbs down into his loving embrace.

I often think of this story when life is bleak because it's like my soul is trapped in the tower, and I need to rescue her . . . but I don't know how. Yet no matter how bad things are, there's always something good about life. And that's the trickle of honey I need to focus on. It could be anything . . . a cloud formation in the sky . . . the distant sound of children laughing . . . a happy memory of being with loved ones.

Often my trickle of honey is the simple sensation of inhaling and exhaling my breath. At first this can seem like a tenuous thread of yum in a world of yuk. But if I stay with my breath, I find myself sinking into the mystery of the moment, and the thread becomes string. If I dive into the mystery, I become conscious of my essential nature, and the string becomes rope. And then my soul is set free from her captivity, and I can embrace her with big love.

The Power of Forgiveness

As I look at the men and women around me in this room, I feel deeply humbled. These seemingly ordinary folk have blown me away. I've met with many remarkable human beings, but this is one of the most extraordinary groups I've ever come across. And what is impressing me so much is that these people have made something good from the most awful situations.

I've been invited to a meeting of the Forgiveness Project, which is a charitable organization that "explores forgiveness, reconciliation, and conflict resolution through real-life human experience." I first came across this wonderful initiative when I was in South Africa, where I met an amazing woman whose daughter had been killed by a bomb during the time of apartheid. What made her so amazing to me was that she now gave presentations on reconciliation alongside the man responsible for the bombing.

Sitting in this circle with me today are people with similar stories. There's a young woman who lost both legs in the 2005 terrorist bombing in London, alongside a young man who used to be a member of a fundamentalist Islamic sect, intent on bloody jihad. There's an Irish woman whose father was killed by an IRA bomb in Northern Ireland, yet she now works with the bomber to heal the wounds of the past. There's also an American woman whose son died in the World Trade Center on 9/11. She now has a strong friendship with a woman whose son is serving a life sentence for conspiring in the attacks, for they recognize the loss and grief they share.

These people are real exemplars of big love. They've experienced the most terrible of losses and have every right to hate and blame. But instead, they have dug deep within their souls to find understanding and compassion. And now they're using the story of their personal suffering to help prevent further suffering for others.

I know from my own experience that it can be very difficult to forgive, and I haven't faced anything remotely as devastating as what these individuals have had to deal with. Sometimes the hurt can be so deep that it seems impossible to forgive, since whenever I think about what has happened, I feel justifiably bitter. But this isn't a comfortable place to be—when I'm bitter, it's hard for life to seem sweet.

The Buddha compared anger to picking up hot coals with the intention of throwing them at someone. That's because when we want to hurt another, we also hurt ourselves. Similarly, when we're consumed with blame, it locks us into the illusion of separateness, and that causes suffering. But when we forgive, this sets us free. And that's why it feels so good to forgive.

If I'm stuck in my story, I find it hard to forgive; but when I'm deep awake, forgiveness is natural. When I'm conscious of the mystery, all of my judgments become open-ended. I can see that my story is just one perspective on life, so I'm able to understand how someone else can see things very differently. And I remember that we were all once innocent children, and at heart we still are. This allows healing to happen because I'm able to hold both my own hurt and the hurt of others within the unconditional embrace of big love.

People often talk about "forgiving and forgetting" as if we need to do both, but that's not always true. It is good to forgive, but we also need to remember the terrible things that we've done to each other so that we don't act in these ways again. What intrigues me is that the bighearted people in this room are able to be both real about their suffering and find forgiveness.

As I sit here in this circle of forgiveness, I feel both the heartbreak of the story and the healing balm of big love. I see that in the story, there are people to praise and others to blame. But in the mystery, there are no judgments. There are no victims or perpetrators. No heroes or villains. No separateness at all. Just communion and compassion.

CHAPTER 15

BECOME
LIKE A CHILD

I've been preparing for a presentation I'm going to give at a conference in Rome on *Jesus and the Lost Goddess,* a book on Gnostic Christianity I wrote with Peter Gandy. I've been flicking through the pages, and I've come across this potent symbol:

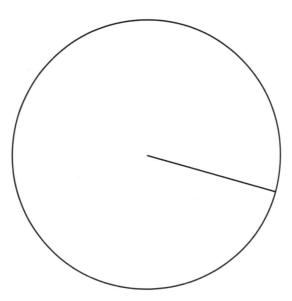

The ancients imagined the self like a circle. The central point represents the "I" of awareness, the circumference represents the body, and the radius represents the psyche. I like this image because I find it helpful to imagine myself like a tree, growing outward from a center and accumulating rings of experience. Over the course of my lifetime, I've accrued more and more concepts with which to navigate my life, and my interior space has gotten larger.

As a child, I accumulated most of my concepts unconsciously through the process of social conditioning. This meant that when I became an adult, I was only partially conscious of what lay within me. I was conscious of the circumference of the circle of self, but unconscious of the inner depths of the psyche.

My journey of awakening has entailed consciously exploring my inner depths. And sporadically during this process, I became unexpectedly conscious of my primal *being* at the center of the circle of self, which had always been there waiting for me to discover it, ever since I was a little baby.

I remember asking my friend Theo Simon how it felt when his daughter was born, since I had loved becoming a father so much. He replied that he was pissed off . . . because clearly his wife had been sleeping with the Buddha! This made me laugh because I knew exactly what he meant.

When I'm around newborn babies, they seem like little Buddhas. This is because the radius of their psyche is so small that we can sense the presence of the oceanic oneness from which they will gradually arise as separate individuals. But babies are not actually spiritual masters, of course. They are unconsciously immersed in the oneness because they don't have the concepts to be conscious yet. They are beginning a journey from unconscious oneness into conscious separateness . . . toward the possibility of conscious oneness.

The adventure of life is a journey into time. As small children, we are totally in the mystery of the moment because we don't have the conceptual apparatus to imagine a past and future. As we mature, we come into time, so we become less present. As our conceptual world becomes more sophisticated, we're able to negotiate the complexities of life, but the price we pay is that we forget the primal simplicity we experienced as children.

Many spiritual traditions encourage us to become like little children again. This is because when we reach back into ourselves, we consciously experience states we inhabited semiconsciously as children. And life becomes timeless, playful, joyous, and dreamlike, as it is for children. We are no longer trapped in our adult story of past and future, so we remember the mystery of the moment.

But, of course, to become *just* like little children again would be disastrous, since we'd be unable to look after ourselves. And that's why adults who only behave like children can be extremely irritating. But we can be conscious of *both* the mundane adult world *and* the magical child's world at the same time. That's living lucidly.

A Natural Awakening

The older I get, the more obvious it becomes that the process we need to go through to wake up and live lucidly is inherent in the natural life process. We come into the world immersed in the unconscious oneness of our essential nature. We become conscious through accumulating concepts that create the world of separateness. By the time we are fully functioning in the adult world, we are ready to become parents—and then into our lives come little beings who remind us of the mystery of the moment, which we have left behind.

This begins a dance in which we teach our children about the conceptual world of separateness, and they entice us back into the playful world of timeless presence. And they demand that we be conscious of both. Children love it when we can be childlike with them, but they also want us to remain responsible adults, able to function in time and protect them from dangers they are not equipped to deal with.

Then as we enter old age, we find it difficult to function in the world of time and begin to inhabit a more childlike state, which is why children often relate better to their grandparents than their parents. In old age, having become conscious through separateness, we are attracted by the stillness and serenity of our essential nature, as we prepare for the climax of the whole adventure, which is death.

This is, of course, an idealized account of the life process. In practice, life is infinitely complex. We all have different journeys and become stuck at different junctures. But I find it fascinating that the natural process of life contains within it the essential blueprint for the journey of awakening.

This suggests to me that this journey is not something we add to our lives. It is the essence of life itself. Waking up is not an activity we engage in alongside other activities, such as making a living and enjoying our hobbies. Awakening is inherent in the natural life process, which is essentially a process of becoming more conscious.

The problem is that for many of us, the process stalls somewhere along the line. By the time we're adolescents, we're usually struggling with the story of separateness, which is why the journey of awakening often begins around this time. But without social support, this early awakening can be short-lived and we're soon pulled into the consensus story by the gravity of our collective unconsciousness.

At some point, something usually happens to shock us awake to the mystery. But once again, this can be short-lived without a supportive community of awakening to nurture our new state of consciousness. Since this is presently lacking in our culture, the result is that most of us become engrossed with the story, which becomes fossilized and fixed. And we enter old age defeated, confused, and terrified by the knowledge that the end of our story is looming.

But the journey of life is a process of continual maturation in which we can always become more conscious. It doesn't end at adulthood. It continues until our last breath. And at any stage in the process, we can step out of the story into the ever-present mystery. The mystery is timeless, so it's never too late. In fact, we can only ever wake up in *this* moment.

Evolution and Regression

I'm driving through the spectacular Rocky Mountains near Boulder, Colorado, with my friend Ed Shapiro. He's a Jewish New Yorker who went to India to explore yoga in the 1960s . . . so I call him

"Swami Eddie." He's playfully wise, refreshingly real, and a little bit mad, and I love him. He's been sharing with me lots of amusing anecdotes from his fascinating life, and his last story has really made me laugh . . . and gotten me thinking.

A few years back, Ed (along with his wonderful wife, Deb) edited a compilation of inspiring essays by various spiritual and cultural celebrities, one of whom was Yoko Ono. Sometime after publication, he received a phone call from a woman asking for Yoko's telephone number because she urgently needed to make contact. Ed politely informed her that he couldn't just hand out a private number, but if she told him why she wanted it, he would see what he could do to help. Reluctantly, the woman told him that she'd been channeling John Lennon and needed to contact Yoko. So Ed innocently suggested, "Why don't you ask John for Yoko's number? He's sure to know it" . . . and she slammed down the phone.

You don't have to spend a long time in spiritual circles to come across people like this woman, who seem lost in a fantasy world, disconnected from the collective one the rest of us inhabit. It seems to me that what's going on here is a form of regression. And it's very common.

The process of awakening entails exploring the depths of our being and becoming like a child. The experience of lucid living arises when we *both* function as an adult in the world *and* play like a child in the mystery. But if we simply abandon the rational adult mind and become childlike, we don't evolve . . . we regress.

Many critics of mysticism, such as Sigmund Freud, treat waking-up experiences as a type of regression to the oceanic oneness of childhood. Sometimes this criticism is justified, for when we abandon the conceptual sophistication of separateness for the simple magic of the moment, we regress to pre-rational states. And this is why some people can be wonderfully spacious and present but hopelessly unable to function properly in the world.

The "child mind" is a magical place to inhabit because it doesn't discriminate between private fantasy and shared reality. When we look at things from a both/and perspective, we can see that the dream of life is both a private fantasy and a shared reality, and we generally keep the two perspectives congruous with each other. But if we abandon the adult discriminating mind, we regress into a personal dream that is cut off from the collective reality.

This is why the rational adult mind is so important. It allows us to differentiate our personal fantasies from our shared reality. We don't want to get trapped in the rational mind, as this can blind us to the magical dimension of life. But we don't want to get trapped in the magical world either, since this leaves us confused and vulnerable . . . and can lead to what we call "insanity."

From what I've seen, regression into the magical world is endemic in modern spirituality. There is a disturbing amount of childlike gullibility, which discredits spirituality among those more rationally sophisticated. Just like a child who can't explain a simple conjuring trick therefore assumes it must be real magic, when *we* can't understand something, we sometimes jump immediately to the most outrageous conclusions.

If we're lost in the magical world, we lose the adult ability to discriminate and question. Then any groundless hunch becomes an intuitive revelation. Personal opinions become absolute truths. And the imaginary friends of childhood become the disembodied masters we are channeling.

I spent a few years in my 20s investigating the phenomenon of channeling. Much channeled "wisdom" is utterly banal, but some of it can be very inspiring. And perhaps sometimes it really is wisdom from a world beyond our own. Who knows? But what concerns me is that I've rarely come across anyone who takes a rational approach to this phenomenon.

I've never found anyone cross-checking information between different channeled entities. I've never found a channeled entity offering to prove the validity of its claims by giving the same message to two different mediums in experimental conditions. If these beings are so spiritually advanced, I would have thought they would have been the first to suggest such rigorous investigation in order to guard against unconscious blind belief. What interests me is that this doesn't happen. And this lack of rational questioning is one of the symptoms of magical regression.

It's a great irony that in the area of spirituality, where we need to be most conscious, we so often regress to a childlike state in which we believe any old nonsense just because we like the sound of it. When we're lost in the magical mind, we become caught up in silly superstitions that we regard as spiritual wisdom. Yet superstitions are hard to avoid because they are so ubiquitous. I even caught myself the other day telling my kids we should "cross our fingers" that it would be sunny when we went to the beach. Beau, who's hot on superstition busting, immediately wanted to know how this would help, exactly.

But I try to keep an open mind on everything. Maybe crossing my fingers does bring good luck? Perhaps it's a ritualized way of framing a positive intention that will lead to the life-dream turning out more favorably for me? But then again, maybe it's just mumbo jumbo? The only way to find out is to investigate it rationally.

And this reminds me of a story that I'm going to share with Swami Eddie, in response to his tale of the woman channeling John Lennon: A street-performer friend of mine was approached after a gig in London by a disheveled woman who asked if he'd like to buy a "lucky" charm. To which he replied with a playful grin, "Well, it doesn't seem to have been very lucky for you!"

Playing in the Child's World

I'm playing with little Aya Sophia, and she's in hysterics because I keep pretending that one of her teddy bears is winking at me when she's not looking. I love being in the child's world with her. In the adult world, things are fixed. But in the child's world, things can turn instantly into other things simply by using the power of the imagination. In the adult world, this teddy bear is a stuffed toy; in the child's world, it's a cheeky friend.

For me, waking up has been a process of learning to enter the child's world as a conscious adult, because it reveals a magical dimension of existence I otherwise miss. The adult mind is rational, pragmatic, serious, responsible, and stable. The child mind is illogical, surreal, playful, irresponsible, and creative. The adult mind is in time, and the child mind is in the moment.

The child mind is the source of art and music, which is why kids have the power to wake us up. When art is rationally dissected, this usually kills it dead, since its role is to take us out of the adult mind and into the poetic imagination. This is the realm inhabited by the mystics when they say things such as: "My heart longs for God like the desert yearns for rain." Taken literally, this is pure nonsense, since deserts don't yearn for anything. But poetically, it conveys a deep truth.

To live lucidly, I need to allow my attention to move between the poetic child mind and the pragmatic adult mind. Right now, for example, I've been playing with Aya Sophia in the child's world, but I really need to start focusing on my adult responsibilities. She's enjoying the present moment, but I'm also conscious of the passage of time. I know she needs to go to bed soon, otherwise she'll be tired for school tomorrow. So it's one more mysterious wink from this teddy, and then it's teeth-cleaning time.

Deep Drugs

The visions have started, and I'm immersed in childlike wonder. . . . As part of my research for a book I'm writing called *Shamanic Wisdomkeepers,* I'm taking part in a service of the Santo Daime, which is a family religion in Brazil. It's a hybrid tradition that combines Catholicism with indigenous Amazonian practices. We've just taken the Eucharist, but it's having more of a transformative effect than I remember from my experiences in the Church of England. And that's because it's laced with ayahuasca, a powerful natural psychedelic drug.

I'm surrounded by a lovely group of people dressed in neat blue and white uniforms, singing unfamiliar hymns to "Our Lady of Conception, the Queen of the Forest." And it feels as if someone has just switched the channel on my inner TV from CNN to the Cartoon Network. Far out! This is like being with the Salvation Army on acid.

People around me are discreetly stepping outside to vomit in paper bags and then returning with a smile. Ayahuasca is seen as a purge that allows us to leave behind negative patterns from the past and have sublime mystical experiences. I don't feel the need to vomit because I've already been through a grueling purge a few days ago, when I spent 13 hours writhing on the floor of a tepee after taking peyote with a Native American shaman. But it was worth it because I emerged in the morning feeling reborn and ecstatic. And now I'm able to enter straight into the ayahuasca experience.

I close my eyes because the visions are enthralling. It doesn't really fit with this "religious" environment, but I seem to be playing an erotic game of hide-and-seek with the Goddess. It's deliciously naughty. I feel so much love. It's like entering a parallel reality and glimpsing a different dimension of life. Yet I know this place. I've been a regular visitor to the intensely beautiful world of the poetic imagination. And I know that many others have made this journey before me.

My sojourn in the visionary world feels timeless, but eventually the Santo Daime ceremony comes to an end and I find myself walking alone through the city night to catch the train home. This amazing event has not been happening in the jungles of Brazil, but in a rented church hall in North London. I wonder what the neighbors would think if they knew.

The visions have stopped, but I'm still in an altered state. And as I'm walking, I'm thinking about the importance of psychedelics, throughout history and in my own life. Men and women have been ingesting psychedelic plants since the earliest times, and such practices are still central to most of the surviving shamanic traditions of the world. Shamanism is the root from which all spirituality has evolved, so it must be acknowledged that taking psychedelic drugs is one of the oldest spiritual practices.

The word "psychedelic" means "soul revealing." I hadn't done any soul-revealing substances for some time before taking the ayahuasca and peyote, but there was a time in my life when this was an important method of waking up. I'm a natural-born explorer of consciousness, so I've been experimenting with psychedelic drugs since my late teens.

I see myself as being in the tradition of a long line of psychedelic explorers, going right back to the earliest shamans and reaching through to modern writers such as Aldous Huxley, Alan Watts, Timothy Leary, Ram Dass, and Terence McKenna; along with a huge number of the artists and musicians whose work has touched me.

Soul-revealing drugs offer a radically different perception of real-ity, in which its dreamlike nature becomes utterly obvious. Right now, for example, as I walk the streets of London, my sensual experience is exaggerated in the most extraordinary way. The night sounds of the city have become like strangely beautiful music, and the pavement I'm walking on is glistening as if inlaid with diamonds.

Terence McKenna compared going to the grave without having had a psychedelic experience to dying a sexual virgin. While this state-ment is deliberately provocative, I know what he means. Exploring the transformative power of psychedelics has been a life-changing experi-ence for me and most of my friends. Indeed, for many people I know, exploring psychedelics gave them their first taste of waking up.

The vast majority of my breakthrough deep awake experiences have not been drug induced, but it seems important to acknowledge that some of them have. Psychedelics catapult me out of my habit-ual mind and into the deep awake state. My sensual experience is so intense that I become very present in the moment. I see the world through new eyes, and my mind is effervescent with insights.

I'll never forget my first LSD trip when I was a teenager because it was one of the most significant events of my life. It felt like going home to the magical world of childhood, in which everything was alive, the colors were vibrant, and the universe was permeated with love. I found myself playing in fairyland. Whatever I paid attention to seemed breathtakingly beautiful and endlessly fascinating.

For me, psychedelics were particularly helpful in my youth, when I was less adept at waking myself up, for they set me free from the con-sensus reality that was threatening to suffocate me. I'd just reached an age when I'd built up a conceptual story about the world, which I needed in order to become an adult. But my concepts were alienating me from the underlying mystery of existence. So taking psychedelics was a way of dismantling my adult conceptual world for a while and reconnecting me with the magical world of childhood, in which I felt really alive and totally free.

In my experience, soul-revealing drugs induce a state of con-sciousness different from the other spiritual techniques I've used to wake myself up. Psychedelics are a doorway into the depths of the magical imagination, but when I become immersed in the magical world, functioning in the practical world becomes extremely difficult. I experience a temporary regression into the child's world of wonder, and this means that I can't engage with the consensus reality.

During my first LSD trip, I remember that a group of us decided we were hungry and should buy some fish and chips from a local shop. But just attempting this simple task in the ordinary world seemed to be the most difficult of challenges. Eventually I went boldly into the shop, which was pulsating with light and color. And, feeling like a naughty child pretending to be a grown-up, I politely asked the man behind the counter for "six portions of salt and vinegar please" . . . then, realizing what I'd said, I ran out of the shop to my waiting friends in fits of laughter.

Becoming so childlike for a while can be immensely liberating and entertaining. But if we continually enter this state, it can lead to permanent regression into the child's world and an inability to be a fully functioning adult. Psychedelics are a great way to glimpse the deep awake state, but to live lucidly, this experience needs to be integrated with the normal waking state. In this way, we're conscious of both the magical child's world and the practical adult's world at the same time.

The Great Taboo

I've always wanted to write about the spiritual use of psychedelics, because the existence of plants and substances that can radically transform consciousness seems extremely significant. But I've avoided doing so for years—it's such a highly charged and complex issue that I've been concerned that what I have to say may be misunderstood.

People could presume that I see "deep drugs" as an essential part of the journey of awakening, which I don't. Or I could be condemned for encouraging young people to break the law, when this is not my intention. In a worst-case scenario, I could find myself being investigated by the police, and my harmless exploration of my own consciousness could end up putting me behind bars.

Discussing the positive power of psychedelics is one of the great taboos of our times. But why is that? And what does it show us about the state of our collective consciousness right now? Drugs can cause terrible suffering, and anyone with a heart would be against drug abuse. But I'm interested in considering what constitutes "use" and "abuse." Like everything in duality, drugs have a positive and a negative aspect. It would be foolish to deny the problems caused by drug *abuse.* But it seems equally foolish to deny the transformative power of drug *use.*

Not everyone who takes deep drugs has a positive experience. And it seems to me that's because people take different drugs for different reasons. Some people want to open themselves up to the magic of life, while others want to escape their suffering. As with everything we do, our intention affects our experience.

When I began experimenting with soul-revealing substances, I had read Aldous Huxley's *The Doors of Perception* and William James's *The Varieties of Religious Experience.* So I was consciously opening myself up to a transcendental experience. And that's exactly what happened. But without this understanding, deep drugs can be little more than a trivial high or, in some cases, disorienting and distressing.

Society doesn't acknowledge the positive power of psychedelics, so when most kids experiment with drugs, they are bereft of guidance. This can mean that what they experience is never properly understood. In the Shamanic traditions, drugs are a spiritual sacrament to be approached with respect. I've always approached psychedelics in this way, so my experiences have been sacred revelations that have changed my life . . . as well as being a lot of childlike fun.

CHAPTER 16

THE END
OF THE STORY

The story of life ends in death, and this seems to make everyone's life ultimately a tragic tale. I have an intuitive conviction that death is not the end, but this doesn't stop the heartbreak of bereavement when someone I love dies. So now I want to explore how living lucidly with big love mitigates the pain of loss and transforms the tragedy of death into a poignantly inspiring experience. Then I want to share with you some profound insights into the nature of life and death, which suggest that, as Rabindranath Tagore puts it:

"Death is not extinguishing the light; it is only putting out the lamp because the dawn has come."

Meeting in the Heartbreak

I'm sitting on the floor surrounded by a circle of people, most of whom are either dying or bereaved, and the room is full of big love. I'm in my late 20s and I'm running a weekend retreat in a beautiful manor house I'm renting. I've moved here from my little pink cottage so that I can host weekends exploring waking up.

Toward the end of my time in my cottage sanctuary, I was full of so much love that I wanted to share that love with others and relieve suffering. The more I found myself waking up to oneness, the more I felt impelled to express my individual nature by making a contribution to the whole. I wanted to be of service.

I guess I was also wondering if the reason I felt so good was because I had found something real, or whether it was simply because I was young, healthy, and carefree; living by a babbling brook; and hanging out in the mystery all day. So I started working with people who were dying or bereaved. I figured that if I spent time around death . . . the ultimate scary monster for most people . . . I would find out if my expanded state of consciousness would collapse when confronted by terrible suffering.

In fact, the opposite has happened. Being with death and loss has awakened me more powerfully than cocooning myself away. And I've found that the love I'm experiencing is big enough to embrace both joy and suffering.

Being immersed in big love is the most wonderful experience I know. Yet love is much more than just a good feeling. It's sharing in the suffering of others as well as the joy. It is caring and fearing and longing and losing. When I think I'm just "Tim," there's so much suffering that it feels impossible to bear. But when I'm deep awake, I can embrace things just as they are.

My work with death and bereavement has led me to run these retreats. And right now I'm sitting in this circle listening to the participants sharing the experiences that have brought them here. There have been some harrowing tales, but the atmosphere is warm and caring. There is a feeling of communion and compassion. Talking about death is waking us up.

The lady who is about to speak is emotional as she tells us about her heroic little boy who died of cancer. He was an inspirational figure who carried on playing soccer even after one of his legs was amputated. She describes sitting with him in the hospital . . . knowing that he was dying . . . and then being given the news that her teenage daughter had just been killed in a car accident.

She stops, and I'm silent because my heart is breaking. There is nothing I can say in the face of such tragedy. There is no philosophy that can mitigate her suffering. Any "wise words" I may attempt would fall like bricks from my mouth. All I can do is be present with her in this moment and invite her into the mystery of big love.

She looks me deeply in the eyes, and it's as if we're hovering above it all, holding the tragedy of life within a limitless embrace. There is an overwhelming feeling of poignancy. In the story, we are suffering; but in the mystery of the moment, everything just is as it is. The suffering is still there, but there's also an unshakable sense that everything is also okay. We are in and out of time together, in the agony and ecstasy of life. We are broken and whole . . . safe and vulnerable . . . and our grief tastes bittersweet.

Death and Love

In my experience, living lucidly with big love mitigates the pain of loss and transforms the tragedy of death into a profoundly meaningful experience. Not long ago, for instance, I heard that my friend Crispin has incurable cancer. He's only 54 and a wonderful man who's full of life . . . so it stinks. I don't want it to be happening. Yet I can't deny that the last few weeks since his remarkable fiancée, Kate, brought him home from the hospital have been truly astonishing.

The tragedy of the situation has brought out the best in everyone. Family and friends have been extraordinary. There's been so much love that it has been overwhelming. There's been a lot of sadness and suffering, too, of course. The love hasn't taken that away, but it has made it deeply poignant. In fact, it has been beautiful.

I've often found that when death calls, people wake up. We come face-to-face with the mystery of existence, and this brings us powerfully into the moment. We begin to realize how precious it is to be alive, despite all there is to complain about. We start to truly appreciate the simple things . . . the perfume of a flower . . . the smile of a friend . . . the stillness of the night. And we start to share our love with one another.

As I've gotten older, death has figured more in my life. It's always painful, yet it always brings out so much love. The loss is only so painful because we love so much, and this love is beautiful, even when it's heartbreaking. The strength of feeling is terrible, but also strangely exhilarating. In the midst of death we can feel intensely alive.

I saw this vividly a few years ago when Peter Gandy's girlfriend, Fran, had a stroke and died unexpectedly. She was a talented painter and only in her 30s. After she died, I spent a few weeks with Peter, and it was an extraordinary time of heartbreaking grief and healing love.

When I heard the news, I immediately traveled to London to be with Peter. When I arrived, we embraced each other, and I said, "I love you." It's not something we often say to each other, but this was a moment for being utterly real. A few minutes later, another friend called, and the first thing he said was "I love you." I had never heard him say this before, but this moment demanded the naked truth.

After her death, it was as if Fran were absent and everywhere. The house became a temporary shrine filled with flowers, and the walls were covered with her astonishing paintings and photos of her life. We organized a beautiful funeral and wake as a celebration of her life and work. At the end, a number of people thanked us for a "great time" . . . and then realized with embarrassment what they had said. But it *was* a great time. How could it not be with that much love in the room? It was awful and awe-ful at the same time.

During this period, Peter became almost shamanic. Just to be in his presence was transformative because he was so present. The past had not gone, since he was full of memories. The future was there as well, since he knew it would be empty of Fran. Yet he was authentically in the now. And although he was haggard with grieving, it was as if he were shining.

When someone leaves this world, it feels as if there's a tear in the fabric of space and time, and we're left distressed and disoriented. Yet through the tear streams the most amazing light, which illuminates all who bathe in it, especially those closest to the tear. I have witnessed this with Crispin and Kate. As the tear in the fabric of reality has widened ominously and Crispin has become more frail and closer to death, he and Kate have been transformed. To be in their presence opens my heart and invites me into the mystery.

I recently had the privilege of helping run a very special evening in their house. A small group of family members and close friends gathered to tell Crispin how much they loved him and to thank him for what he had given them. It was an incredibly moving experience . . . especially listening to the teenage children in the room find words for their feelings. We connected more completely in those few hours than many people do in a whole lifetime.

And then Kate and Crispin decided to get married, as they had often talked of doing. Friends rallied to make arrangements in what seemed an impossibly short time, and we had a wonderful ceremony in their favorite village church, followed by a pilgrimage up a hill to a local beauty spot. Crispin sat in stately honor on a sedan chair, created by friends who carried him up the hill. And here we built a fire, around which we ate and drank and talked and laughed. Crispin was serenely happy, and I said to him with a wicked smile,

> "You know, if you'd lived to be 80 you wouldn't have all these beautiful women fussing around you and guys carrying you up a hill. You'd be just another one falling through the net."

The strange thing is that my wife, Debbie, had foreseen this day in a dream a year before, when she'd seen herself at a party on a hill with Crispin lying on some sort of bed. I've often found that around death, bizarre things happen, which feel significant even if I don't know why. On two occasions after a close friend has died, I've woken in the night to find bats flying about in my bedroom. I don't know what it meant, but it was both alarming and somehow reassuring.

Life can become very dreamlike when we're dancing with death, as if what happens is revealing some hidden pattern to life. When Fran died, she had just come back from a trip to Mexico with Peter, during which time she had visited the house of the artist Frida Kahlo. Fran felt very connected to Frida. And then, like Frida, she died young, just as her work was beginning to command real respect. She didn't know that one of her best friends had recently done the voice-over for a documentary on Kahlo. But it felt meaningful that the program was televised the night of Fran's wake. Yet what it meant, I couldn't say.

Death with Style

Crispin only has a few days to live, so I've come over to say goodbye. The living room, which is next to Crispin's "dying room," is full of people talking warmly. But the silence seems louder. This average terraced house has become a sacred space, vibrating with energy and presence. And this is all because of someone in the next room who's doing nothing much, as he's too feeble to even leave his bed.

While waiting to go in to see the man himself, I'm flipping through some amazing pictures taken yesterday of Crispin covered in sticky blue slime. A few days ago he'd heard that a member of Alabama 3, one of his favorite bands, had started making bronze death masks as they used to do in ancient times. Kate had found a way to make contact with this guy, and yesterday he'd come to make a mask of Crispin in his last days.

As you'd expect, when Crispin first had to face his imminent death, it was a terrifying shock. But he's been a lifelong explorer of consciousness and an adventurer in the world of psychedelics. So when a friend suggested that he now had to let go into the trip, just as he had done so many times before, Crispin knew the way to be with what was happening. And now he's doing death with style.

As I come into his room, Crispin is propped up in bed, surrounded by books he's reading, looking thin and frail. But he also looks translucent, as if there's a light mysteriously shining through him. Kate had told me that the nearer Crispin has gotten to death, the more himself he has become . . . and I can see that she is right.

I take his fragile hand in mine and look into his clear eyes. Then I say,

"So, Crispin, you're dying . . . what's it like?"

His reply is a beatific smile. And then he says conspiratorially,

"To tell you the truth, I'm enjoying it."

○ ○ ○

CHAPTER 17

DEATH IS
WAKING UP

I've been listening to a dance track I recorded in my early 30s called "Another Level of Fun," which features an amusing rap by Ram Dass about waking up. The track climaxes with him leading a meditation into the moment, against a driving didgeridoo. And it ends with him nonchalantly saying . . . "Death is absolutely safe." To which he cheekily adds . . . "Doesn't that give a new meaning to the word 'safe'?!"

One of the most reassuring teachings of spirituality is that we don't need to fear death, since the ending of one story is a transition into a new story. But is this true, or is the self "use once and throw away"? How I answer this question really affects how I feel about life. Especially now that I'm getting older!

What is death? This is a koan I've been contemplating for years. A *koan* is a Zen term for a question that can lead to a profound transformation of consciousness. When I work with a koan, I turn it over in my mind and let it sink into my unconscious depths. Sometime later, there's often a rush of new insights. When this happens, I consider these insights with the rational mind; if they make sense, I embrace them, provisionally at least. Especially if I also find them beautiful.

Up until recently, however, my years of contemplating the koan "What is death?" hadn't led to any genuine insight, and I was beginning to feel that they never would. All I really knew was that in the deep awake state, I had no fear of death, because I found myself overwhelmed by big love and a profound sense that everything is okay just as it is . . . including death.

But a few months ago, I unexpectedly experienced a burst of insight that has convinced me that Ram Dass is right . . . death is safe. These ideas arose while I was examining the familiar states of consciousness we experience every day . . . deep sleep, dreaming, and waking . . . as well as the ultraconscious deep awake state. So before I explore my insights about death, I need to share how I came to what I call "the Russian-dolls theory of consciousness."

States of Consciousness

What is the relationship between different states of consciousness? The first thing that strikes me is very simple . . .

In the dreaming state, I'm more conscious than in deep sleep.

In the waking state, I'm more conscious than when I dream.

In the deep awake state, I'm more conscious than in the waking state.

When I examine these states more closely, I see that with each expansion of consciousness, I experience reality in a different way:

In the dreaming state, I have no idea that I am dreaming, and the dreamworld appears "real."

In the waking state, I see that my dreamworld was imaginary, and the waking world seems "real."

In the deep awake state, I see that the waking world is also not what it seems, for life is like a collective dream.

These changes in my understanding of reality are accompanied by a greater degree of self-knowledge:

In the dreaming state, I believe that I'm my dream persona.

In the waking state, I believe that I'm my waking persona, and I see my dream persona as a figment of my individual imagination.

In the deep awake state, I realize that I'm the presence of awareness, and I see my waking persona as an expression of the primal imagination, which is one with all.

The question that arises from these observations is this: if it's possible to be deep awake, why do we also have to inhabit the deep sleep, dreaming, and waking states?

I feel that I can answer this question by making use of the idea that reality is comprised of "holons." The concept of a "holon" was coined by the British philosopher Arthur Koestler and developed by the American philosopher Ken Wilber.

A holon is a whole/part. It is a whole made up of parts, which is also a part of a greater whole. This sentence is a holon because it's a whole made up of words and a part of this paragraph.

Every object in the universe is a holon because everything is a whole made up of parts, which are in turn wholes made up of parts. Your body is a holon because it is a whole made of up cells, which are wholes made up of molecules, which are wholes made of atoms, and so on.

Holons can be seen as Russian dolls nested within each other, with the greater holons being predicated on the lesser holons they contain. You can't have cells without atoms or bodies without cells. You can't have a paragraph without sentences, sentences without words, or words without letters. Life is characterized everywhere by hierarchies of holons or "holarchies."

What is intriguing me is the possibility that the different states of consciousness we inhabit form a holarchy, in which the higher states are predicated on the lower states. To be in the waking state, we need to also inhabit the less conscious dreaming and deep sleep states from time to time. Likewise, to inhabit the deep awake state, we need to experience all of the other states on which it is predicated.

Consciousness is a holarchy of states, and I need to experience the lesser in order to sustain the greater states . . .

If I didn't rest in the unconsciousness of deep sleep, I'd never be conscious at all . . . and this is why when I've deliberately gone without sleep, I've eventually passed out.

If I didn't experience the personal fantasies of my dreams, I wouldn't be able to function in the shared waking world . . . and this is why when I've stayed awake for long periods, I've started to hallucinate, as my dreams impose themselves on my attention.

If I didn't experience the shared waking world, I wouldn't be able to become conscious of my essential nature, which is one with all . . . and this is why I have to keep focusing on the practicalities of the waking state that sustain my existence, not just space out into deep awake wonder.

Higher states of consciousness are predicated on lower states of consciousness. This is why we regularly pass from the ground of unconscious awareness, up through the dreaming state, to the waking state . . . and beyond to the deep awake state. It's impossible to stay permanently in the deep awake state because it's built upon the lesser states, which we also need to inhabit from time to time. The ecstasy of higher consciousness is predicated on the practical waking state, the private dreaming state, and the rest of deep sleep. And we need to allow our focus to pass fluidly between all of these states.

The Koan Pops!

I'm puttering about in my office when I'm suddenly flooded with insights. My death koan has unexpectedly erupted into a flood of realizations, which I find both rational and beautiful. And they're helping me see the traditional spiritual teachings about death in a completely new way. Astonishing!

At a seminar a few years ago, a gentleman asked me, "If life is like a dream, what happens when you die?" I replied, "I don't know. Have you ever died in a dream?" The gentleman answered, "Actually, I have." So I said, "What happened?" He said, "I woke up." Then he added, "I think I may have answered my own question," which made everybody laugh.

The rush of insights I am experiencing is making me take this little joke seriously. It seems to me that the relationship between the after-death state and the waking state is comparable to the relationship between the waking state and the dreaming state. We pass between the after-death state and the life state, just as we do between the waking state and the dreaming state.

Earlier when I was exploring the holarchy of states of consciousness, I saw that higher states of consciousness are predicated on lower states of consciousness. To be in the waking state, I need to also inhabit the dreaming and deep sleep states. Perhaps there's a higher state of consciousness that we wake up to after death, which is predicated on our also entering the life states from time to time?

Those who have had "near-death experiences" describe an all-consuming oneness and unconditional love in the after-death state. It seems to me that this is because the after-death state is being fully deep awake. In the waking state, we're forever struggling with separateness. But in the after-death state, we know that essentially all is one, so we bathe in the bliss of big love. *use it!*

Life is a necessary precursor to the after-death state, just as dreaming is a necessary precursor to the waking state. We have to explore our personal fantasies in the dream state in order to be conscious of ourselves as separate individuals in the waking state. And we have to explore our separate nature in the waking state in order to be conscious of our essential oneness in the after-death state.

To be awake, I have to have been asleep & deep asleep
To wake up after death, I have to have been in 189
certain life states
("Life" is a prep. for after death experience)

after death

Dying is not perpetual unconscious sleep. It's a further waking up to a higher state of consciousness, which is predicated on the lesser states of consciousness. Deep sleep is the ground from which consciousness expands, through the dreaming state to the waking state, and then to the after-death state.

This realization casts my experience of lucid living in a new light. I can see that when I dream lucidly, I'm conscious enough to remember something of the waking state while dreaming. And it now seems to me that when I live lucidly, I'm conscious enough to remember something of the after-death state of big love while I'm living.

(remembering myself)

Conscious Oneness

I feel philosophically excited because these new insights are transforming my understanding of my own identity. The ancients believed that although we appear to be mere mortals, in reality we are "daemons" or immortal gods. Jesus famously quotes Psalm 82, which paradoxically proclaims, "You are gods . . . but you shall die like men." It's an outrageous claim, but suddenly I feel that I know what it means.

I have many levels to my individuality. In a dream, I appear to be my dream persona. In the waking state, I appear to be my life persona. It seems to me that there is a yet more conscious level of my individuality, and this is my daemon.

higher level My daemon is dreaming itself to be "Tim" in the same way that Tim dreams himself to be his dream persona. But this higher level of my individuality is consciously one with all, so the dream my daemon is dreaming is an individual perspective on the shared dream of life.

These insights are helping make sense of the feeling I've often had that I'm growing toward some preexistent higher self, which I'm attempting to embody. And they are helping me understand my persistent intuition that death is not the end.

Previously, I'd been conscious of my deeper identity as the impersonal oneness of awareness, but I'd seen the ultimate expression of my individuality as Tim. I hadn't properly considered the idea that my individuality could take a deeper form. This meant that I was puzzled by death.

I used to feel that death was waking up to my deeper nature. So I imagined that when I died, my apparent nature as Tim disappeared, but my essential nature as the oneness of awareness continued. This left me with a problem, since consciousness arises with separateness. So *just* surviving as the primal awareness would amount to being in a permanent state of deep sleep. And I don't find this idea very attractive.

If death is dissolving back into the one, like a drop of water returning to the sea, it makes having been the drop seem meaningless. This doesn't feel right to me, as the individual self is so precious. It doesn't make sense that the process of accumulating experience and wisdom during this lifetime is ultimately futile.

But when I see that I have a higher level to my individuality, all of these problems evaporate. Death is not the end of my individuality. My nature is always characterized by polarity. I am always *both* an individual *and* one with all.

My individuality expresses itself in different ways in the dreaming, waking, and after-death states. Tim is a level of my individuality that is struggling to become conscious enough to see through separateness. My daemon is a level of my individuality that knows I am an individual expression of the primal oneness of awareness.

This is helping me understand the analogy between lucid dreaming and lucid living in a new way. When I dream lucidly, I'm partially conscious of the waking state while I'm dreaming. When I live lucidly, I'm partially conscious of the after-death state while I'm living. Being deep awake is a tantalizing taste of being a fully conscious daemon.

Heaven and Reincarnation

Suddenly the idea of heaven, which is ubiquitous in spiritual literature, seems more than a wish-fulfilling fantasy. A higher state of being in which we are consciously one in big love would indeed be heavenly.

I used to have a problem with the idea of a heavenly afterlife because it seemed to make this life pointless. If it's possible to experience heaven, why don't we go straight there? We're told that life is some sort of testing ground to see if we deserve to enter through those pearly gates. But I don't like this idea. If life is an entrance examination, it's certainly not a fair one, because the obstacles we face in our lives are so diverse.

From my new perspective, I don't have this problem. Life is not an entrance exam for the after-death state, just as dreaming is not an entrance exam for the waking state. We naturally pass between all of these states because they are different levels in the holarchy of consciousness.

This is helping me understand the idea of reincarnation, which previously didn't make sense to me. I felt that there was something meaningless about surviving as someone else if I didn't remember anything about Tim. But the idea of a holarchy of consciousness casts reincarnation in a different light.

In the same way that we have to return to the dreaming and deep sleep states to sustain the waking state, we have to return to the life experience of separateness to sustain the after-death experience of oneness. All of these states are essential to the evolution of consciousness.

My individual nature is a holarchy, with higher levels of my individuality transcending and including the lower levels. Right now I appear to be "Tim." And this level of my identity transcends and includes all of my different dream personas, which I know to be aspects of Tim. In the same way, the daemon in the after-death state is a deeper level of my individuality, which transcends and includes Tim, who is now seen as one of many life personas the daemon has dreamed itself to be.

Socrates claimed that death is remembering, not forgetting. This now makes sense because the more conscious I become, the more I remember.

The ground of being is the deep sleep state in which I remember nothing.

In the dreaming state, I have some memories, but I don't remember the waking state.

In the waking state, I can recall both my dreams and waking experiences, but mostly I forget both.

This suggests that in the ultraconscious after-death state, I remember much more than I do now.

Those who have had near-death experiences often report total recall of what has happened in their lives, which they review from a detached perspective. Is this because in the after-death state we can remember our lives and learn from them, just as we can remember and learn from our dreams in the waking state?

Exile and Home

Now I understand why I experience a sense of being an alien in this world. Ever since I was a child, life has seemed immensely strange to me, and I've often wondered why. If this is all I've ever known, life should feel familiar, not strange. Perhaps the explanation is that this life is *not* all I've ever known.

I sometimes find a dream strange when something "impossible" occurs, since I vaguely remember the waking state in which this sort of thing doesn't happen. Perhaps in the same way, I find life strange because I have deep memories of the after-death state, in which I don't experience the conflicts that arise from separateness.

In my poetic imagination, I've often thought of life as a journey home. It's a common theme in mystical literature. We are presently exiled from our true abode, to which we are returning. This now seems like a vivid reality to me. Death is going home.

I used to worry that death rendered life ultimately meaningless. But now it feels as if life is actually redeemed by death. When the dream of life becomes a nightmare, I can remember that one day I'll wake up and realize that everything is okay. When I feel most lost, I can be reassured that I'll eventually find my way home.

These new insights that have exploded from the koan "What is death?" have left me accepting Tim's inevitable demise. And this makes me feel good about life because I see that there's all this . . . *and death, too!* It seems to me now that Walt Whitman was right when he provocatively claimed:

"To die is different from what any one supposed, and luckier."

CHAPTER 18

HOW LONG
IS NOW?

When we dive deeply into the deep awake state, we become conscious of our essential nature as the daemon or spirit. This doesn't exist within the dream of life; it is the life-dreamer itself. So I want to complete our journey of awakening together by helping you fully appreciate something truly astonishing:

Your essential being does not exist in time and space.

I want to invite you to contemplate two powerful koans with me, which will forever change your understanding of who you are. I'm going to share with you the insights that arise for me, and I invite you to check out my insights to see if they are true in your own experience.

What I want to show you is so far beyond our normal way of looking at things that it can seem difficult to grasp at first, so take your time. Really focus on the question and pay attention to the reality of the moment. The more you look, the more you'll see.

HOW LONG IS NOW?

I'm paying attention to the moment, looking for clues, but it seems to be an impossible question to answer.

HOW LONG IS NOW?

If I look at it one way, it's obvious that "now" is an instant so short I can't measure it. It's gone before I've had time to register it.

HOW LONG IS NOW?

But if I look at it another way, it's always now. Now is forever. The present is timeless.

HOW LONG IS NOW?

Now is too brief to grasp and so constant that it has no beginning or end.

HOW LONG IS NOW?

Right now I'm awareness witnessing a flow of thoughts and sensations. The appearances are in permanent flux, which is why the moment seems so brief that I can't catch it.

HOW LONG IS NOW?

My experiences are changing all the time. Indeed, "time" is what we call the ever-changing appearances.

HOW LONG IS NOW?

But if I focus my attention on my essential nature as awareness, I see that it has the polar-opposite quality. Awareness is

[handwritten: can't be of time]

a constant presence that is always present. It never changes because it has no qualities that could change.

HOW LONG IS NOW?

Awareness is a continual stillness witnessing all the changes. Awareness is not in time. Awareness is witnessing time. This is why the moment seems eternal.

HOW LONG IS NOW?

[handwritten: "Jane" in Time → eternity / timeless / essential nature (awareness) witnessing]

Now is a polarity. Now is the coexistence of time and eternity. Now is impossibly transient, and it goes on forever.

HOW LONG IS NOW?

Tim is a person in time, but my essential nature is the timeless presence of awareness.

When the mystics talk about the experience of "eternal life" and "timeless eternity," it can sound like something amazing that we may experience when we die. But the experience of eternity is actually always available to us here and now. In the normal waking state, we're immersed in time, but when we pay attention to our essential nature as awareness, we become deep awake in the timeless moment.

Now-here and Nowhere

Let's go even deeper by contemplating another powerful koan together. I'll report my insights just like before, and I invite you to check them out in your own experience. Once again, it's important not to hurry. Really pay attention to the moment. If you do, you will find that your world turns inside out . . . literally. And that's quite a rush!

WHERE IS AWARENESS?

I am conscious of myself as the "I" of awareness witnessing this moment, but where is the "I"?

WHERE IS AWARENESS?

Usually I think of awareness as existing inside my head. But this simply isn't true. If I asked someone to crack open my skull and take a look, they'd never find awareness. Not even if they looked with a microscope. It's just not there. My head is full of brains, but awareness is nowhere to be found.

WHERE IS AWARENESS?

Clearly, awareness doesn't exist inside my skin.

WHERE IS AWARENESS?

It's not something I can sense or imagine . . . and it doesn't exist in time.

WHERE IS AWARENESS?

Awareness can't be found in my experience, so where the hell is it?

WHERE IS AWARENESS?

As I examine the moment, it seems to me that awareness is nowhere and everywhere.

WHERE IS AWARENESS?

Awareness isn't within my experience, since my experience is within awareness.

WHERE IS AWARENESS?

The world is arising within awareness like a dream.

WHERE IS AWARENESS?

Everything that I'm experiencing right now exists within awareness. (becg I exist w/in awareness) as Jane

WHERE IS AWARENESS?

My thoughts exist within awareness; if they didn't, I wouldn't be conscious of them. My sensations exist within awareness; if they didn't, I wouldn't be conscious of them. Tim exists within awareness; if he didn't, I wouldn't be conscious of him.

WHERE IS AWARENESS?

I'm the spacious presence of awareness, and Tim is an appearance that exists within me.

WHERE IS AWARENESS?

Awareness is an emptiness that contains the world. And this is why the Buddhists say that to know our true Buddha-nature is to experience the void of *nirvana* within which the appearances of *samsara* are arising.

WHERE IS AWARENESS?

As I contemplate this koan, something extraordinary is happening. . . .

Everything is becoming incredibly simple, and I can see that this moment is characterized by the polarity of awareness and appearances . . . emptiness and form . . . nirvana and samsara . . . life-dreamer and life-dream.

awareness   appearances
emptiness   ∆   fullness - form   199
stillness   movement
dreamer   dream

I have reduced my appreciation of life to the polar simplicity of spacious awareness and the appearances it contains.

Now everything is going into slow motion . . . and the two become one.

It feels as if the moment has frozen into a pulsating stillness.

Awareness is one with the flow of appearances, just as space is one with the objects it contains.

The dreamer is one with the dream.

I'm not separate from what I'm experiencing.

All is one . . . and I am that oneness.

The "I" Door

I'd like to contemplate the present moment once more with you, because I want to explore how the "I" of awareness is like a doorway out of time and separateness . . . and into eternity and oneness. I'm going to do this now and describe what I experience—and, as before, I invite you to make the journey with me.

As I pay attention to the "I," it feels as if I'm withdrawing within and separating myself from the world . . . my personality . . . everything.

I am retreating into the center of my being, which is such an impossibly small point that I can't find it.

And then in a sudden reality shift, the world turns inside out, and I'm an emptiness that contains everything.

What just happened?! A moment ago the "I" was an impossibly small point within . . . now the "I" is a spacious, timeless nothing.

The "I" is like a wormhole in the time-space continuum . . . which leads from here and now to everywhere and always.

It's like a secret doorway out of the appearances and into the mystery.

On one side of the "I" door is oneness, and on the other side is separateness.

On one side of the "I" door, I'm the primal awareness, and on the other side, I'm this person known as Tim.

On one side of the "I" door, I'm the life-dreamer, and on the other side, I am a character in the life-dream.

On one side of the "I" door, everything is just perfect as it is; and on the other side, I'm a player in the great evolutionary story of one and all, which is full of joy and suffering, heroism and cruelty, hope and despair. A story that is propelling us ever onward to our collective awakening.

If you get this grand vision, it will transform your life. If it seems elusive, keep being conscious of being conscious—I assure you that sooner or later, you'll pass through the "I" door, and the world will turn inside out. Then you might want to remember this little poem by the Sufi sage Rumi, as it will make you smile:

> "They said knock and the door will open,
> I knocked . . . the door opened,
> and I found I'd be knocking from the inside."

become conscious of being conscious

○ ○ ○

In in + out at the same time

CHAPTER 19

A DEEP
AWAKE WORLD

I've been watching the spectacular closing ceremony of the 2008 Summer Olympics. It's inspiring to see the nations of the world meeting in peace and harmony in Beijing, even when they're busy fighting elsewhere. Sports are wonderful examples of how we can honor both our oneness and our separateness by competing in a spirit of cooperation. And the slogan for the games could not have been better: "One World, One Dream."

Yet part of me can't help but see this slogan as ironic, given the repressive nature of the Chinese regime and the relentless political self-interest displayed by most of the other competing countries. But such a beautiful vision is wonderful nevertheless. It speaks to our deep aspiration for harmony, although we have little idea how we can make this vision an actuality.

Our world is very beautiful but extremely messed up. We face so many seemingly insurmountable problems . . . insane wars, dire poverty, environmental catastrophes, religious bigotry, divisive nationalism, predatory big business, rampant AIDS, endemic stress, existential meaninglessness, political small-mindedness, and so on. There's so much that needs doing that it's easy to feel overwhelmed and pessimistic.

We tolerate the obscene fact that the richest two hundred people own more wealth than the bottom four billion do. We equate happiness with crass consumerism, even though we know in our hearts that this is not making us happier. In many places we're still working out conflicts that arise from grudges going back centuries, which we just will not let go of. And the people in positions of power in politics and business are usually asleep in separateness and self-serving.

Sometimes I feel like old Lao-tzu, who became so sick of the ways of men that he saddled up his water buffalo and rode off into the west. Then I find myself responding to the "bad news" on TV with, "Saddle up my water buffalo!"

Like most people, I want the world to be a better place. I've never felt at home here—it's as if I could remember some other world in which cruelty and callousness weren't so common. I was a child in the 1960s and picked up on the sudden expansion of consciousness that happened then, along with the euphoric optimism that accompanied it. Since then, as I've woken up to oneness and big love, my empathy with the suffering of others has grown, and my longing for a deep awake world has become more acute.

I don't see a "deep awake world" as some utopian state of heaven on earth. The life-dream is predicated on polarity, so there will always be joy and suffering. There will always be some people who are more conscious than others. There will always be problems that need to be solved. But I can easily envision a world in which the majority of humanity is familiar with the deep awake state, so we live together in communion and with compassion. And that is the world I would like to call home.

In my teens, I expected that by the time I was in my 40s I would have seen the world profoundly transformed. But this hasn't happened. Yet what *has* happened is that more and more people have been quietly waking up. And for me, this is cause for genuine hope. Because I can see that the only way we will really deal with the endless problems that seem to afflict us is to evolve into a new collective consciousness.

Einstein put things succinctly when he said, "We cannot solve our problems with the mind that created them." To change the world, we need to see more deeply into the nature of reality. We need to think in new ways. We need to develop a new story to live by, which is grounded in the realization that we are all one. We need to understand that the quality of our lives is governed primarily by how conscious we are, not by how much we possess or how important we become. We need to transform our collective state of consciousness.

Like Einstein and so many other pioneers of the new edge, Gandhi also believed that ultimately, only a change of consciousness would create a better world. He urged us to "be the change" we want to see in the world. Consciousness can only be transformed person by person. And our greatest contribution is to wake ourselves up and live in a new way. To become what I call "ambassadors for oneness," who bring the new world of big love into being by living there now and sharing it with others. And if being an "ambassador" sounds too extroverted, we can become "secret agents for love" and do the same work, but anonymously undercover.

States of consciousness are catching, so the more of us who wake up to oneness, the easier it becomes for others to wake up. And this can happen to anyone at any time . . . rich or poor, powerful or defenseless, oppressor or oppressed. If enough of us come to understand that we are one, the oppressive status quo of institutionalized self-interest will overthrow itself, for it's only a symptom of the sickness of separateness. And this is healed the moment we become deep awake.

During the First World War, in the midst of the squalor and terror of the trenches, German and British soldiers stopped butchering each other one Christmas Day and played soccer together instead. Something about the magic of Christmas allowed them to see that what really divided them was no more substantial than an "idea." One set of young men had the idea of being "German" and the other of being "British." Defining their identities by these ideas had led them to inflict the most terrible suffering on each other. But for one day they were able to see through the veil of separateness and play together.

What would happen if *every* day we could see through what seemingly divides us and recognize that we are essentially one? What would happen if we were no longer attached to the labels that define our differences and instead allowed the divisions between us to evaporate? Maybe we'd stop killing each other and start playing together instead. Perhaps we could make it like Christmas Day in the trenches every day.

The solution to our problems is love. This idea is nothing new, of course. Wise men and women have been telling us that love is the answer for millennia, and deep down most of us know this to be true. It is preached from the pulpit in churches, mosques, and temples. We hear it every day on the radio in countless uplifting songs. Yet still our culture treats this perennial wisdom as naïve sentimentality for people who don't live in the "real world." But the opposite is true. It is those who dismiss the transformative power of love who aren't living in the real world.

Separateness is predicated on nothing more substantial than a concept. We believe that we are separate, and all of our misguided actions arise from this one error. If we could replace this mistake with an understanding of our essential oneness, we could create a deep awake world full of lucid individuals. A world of communion and compassion, liberty and love, self-expression and service, me and we.

The Evolution of Us

We cause ourselves so much unnecessary suffering that it's hard to bear. There's a temptation to give up and go numb. But something in me refuses this easy answer, since the price is my passion for life. I long to live in a world of compassion and justice, so when I look at all of the cruelty and injustice, it can fill me with despair. Yet when I embrace a deeper understanding of the human predicament, I see that my pessimism is unfounded because the present state of the world is an inevitable product of our gradual evolution.

We are unconscious nature becoming conscious. So when human beings behave in cruel and barbaric ways, they are simply being natural. There's no compassion in unconscious nature, which is predicated on the struggle for survival. There's no justice in nature, where the innocent suffer and the guilty flourish. It's the development of consciousness that introduces the possibility of compassion and justice into the evolutionary process.

Through the evolution of humanity, unconscious nature is becoming compassionate. The present evils of human society are to be expected because we're still so collectively immersed in unconscious nature. War between nations is simply the continuation of the process that nature has used to sort the weak from the strong since the beginning of life. Predatory big business is founded on the profit motive ubiquitous in nature.

Narrow human self-interest is a natural by-product of our evolution through separateness. Yet with the emergences of higher forms of consciousness, we're able to reflect on this unconscious natural process and change how we choose to go about things. With greater consciousness comes greater communion, which is the source of greater compassion. So the more conscious we are, the kinder we become.

When we empathize with each other, we can't help but want to ameliorate suffering . . . to which nature is indifferent. And to care for the disadvantaged . . . whom nature rejects. And to protect endangered species . . . that nature would write off. We want to be of service to others . . . because we've transcended the natural desire for personal profit.

From an evolutionary perspective, the problems of the modern world may be blessings in disguise because they are pushing us to become deep awake. Environmental degradation, rampant AIDS, religious terrorism, rapacious big business . . . are all global problems that we can only solve by working together. And this is propelling us to make the next evolutionary leap by waking up to oneness and big love.

The idea of a collective awakening can seem like an unrealistic fantasy, since there's a weariness in our culture. We're cynical about the possibility of a brighter future. We feel disempowered and impotent. And this is because we're living in what I call the "Age of Disillusionment."

We are becoming disillusioned with dogmas and ideologies because they've been so divisive. We're becoming disillusioned with our political leaders because so many have been revealed as self-seeking hypocrites. We're becoming disillusioned with the media because we see that it tells us lies. We're becoming disillusioned with religion because unspeakable horrors are carried out in its name. We're becoming disillusioned with science because its great advances have led to weapons of mass destruction and environmental disaster. We're even becoming disillusioned with consumerism because our modern riches have not made us happier.

Becoming cynical can lead to pessimism and apathy. But it seems to me that the Age of Disillusionment is the necessary prequel to a deep awake world. We need to see through these illusions if we are to discover that the only genuine solution to our problems is to change our state of consciousness.

At the moment, a collective awakening may not seem much in evidence—it's a possibility only taken seriously by a relatively small number of people who think outside the box. But this should not surprise us. History shows us that great ideas . . . artistic, philosophical, political, scientific . . . come from those who are first dismissed as heretics. The harbingers of change are always marginalized. To be on the cutting edge is, by definition, to be a minority. If we want to see where the future is being born, we need to look to those who are presently on the edge.

If enough of us joined the "new edge tribe," we'd have a deep awake world. But for that to happen, more of us have to step out of the "story of me" and engage with the "story of us." And the "story of us" is a grand tale of the evolution of awareness from unconscious oneness, through conscious separateness, to conscious oneness.

Scientists have concluded that the human race has evolved from a handful of common ancestors . . . who evolved from more primitive forms of life . . . which evolved from inanimate matter . . . which evolved from the spectacular burst of creativity that arose from what scientists call the "singularity." We are the singularity becoming conscious of itself.

Human beings are the avant-garde cosmic art form because we're distinguished by a remarkable new development. We are not only conscious . . . we are conscious that we are conscious. Yet most of us are so enamored with the delights and dramas of our sensual experience that we pay little attention to the mysterious "I" that is witnessing them. But when we do, we become deep awake. Then we see that in reality, all is one, and we start to live lucidly in love.

Things have changed substantially since the mysterious nothing first manifested as something. Simple gases have developed into vast galaxies of stars. Inanimate matter has evolved into multifarious life-forms, through which the cosmos has come to see, hear, and touch itself. After billions of years, here we are . . . self-conscious human beings. And when I feel the weight of deep history pushing us forward, I realize how far we have come and how far we could go.

Becoming Part of the ALL

I've been addressing a gathering of the Alliance for Lucid Living, and I'm drawing our time together to a close. The ALL is a worldwide alliance of individuals who share a passion for living lucidly. It exists to nurture the development of the new tribe arising at the cutting edge of evolution. This tribe is united by consciousness, not locality, so it is difficult to bring together. But this is gradually happening. There are ALL gatherings being organized in various global locations. And the Internet is offering novel ways to build a genuine community of awakening individuals.

I decide to end my presentation with an open invitation to people to become personally committed to forwarding our collective awakening:

"We all get to make a contribution to the shared adventure we call 'life' by expressing our own idiosyncratic nature. My contribution as a philosopher is to add my voice to those attempting to articulate a new spiritual philosophy, fresh enough to capture the modern imagination and powerful enough to actually wake us up.

"But I see that this is not enough. We need a community of awakening to nurture our personal and collective transformation. My contribution here has been to set up the ALL. It aims to be a forum for supporting each other, sharing our insights and creative endeavors, and introducing the deep awake state to anyone interested in exploring the mystery of existence.

"To create a deep awake world, we need to truly live lucidly in love, not just think about it. The ALL can offer us the inspiration we need to do just that. So we can dive into the great adventure of evolution together. And each play our part with passion in the great pageant of life.

"Is it really possible that a significant transformation in collective consciousness could happen? Of course it is. Look at the world around us. It's a miracle of infinite proportions. Anything is possible. And that is why I want to invite you become a part of the ALL and work with us to create a deep awake world.

"I don't say this because I have some apocalyptic vision of an imminent transformation. Some people believe that a revolution in consciousness will just happen, due to mysterious 'Earth changes' or the ending of the Mayan calendar in 2012. But I suspect that this is just magical regression and wishful thinking.

"In reality, the change will only come as we learn to embody big love and live lucidly. And while we can make this transformation individually in a moment, collectively it will probably take too long for us to see a deep awake world in our own lifetimes. This work of forwarding our collective awakening is a compassionate gift to the generations that will come after us. It is our legacy to the future.

"So I urge you to think about your death and then ask yourself what it is you want to do with your life. What do you want to be and do and share before you take your bow and leave the stage? How do you want to use the resources of time, talent, and money available to you? What does the oneness of our essential nature want to contribute through you?

"Here we are on a journey from birth to death, with an opportunity to contribute a verse to the song of life. I want to sing of a deep awake world. I want to sing of a new tribe of compassionate, creative, wise, liberated, erotic, sublime, appreciative, unique individuals, living lucidly as one and many.

"If you do, too, let's sing together and raise the roof."

CHAPTER 20

THE FOOL
ON THE HILL

I'm sitting on Summerhouse Hill, overlooking the town of my birth. This is where my adventure of awakening began when I was a 12-year-old boy. The hill is the same, but the view has changed. Back then I looked down upon the old station where I would catch a steam train with my father before school, just for the fun of it. Now I see an entertainment complex where I take my kids bowling with their friends.

I've been here for some hours watching the evening become the night. I don't really know why I've come back. Perhaps to reconnect with that young boy I once was? Perhaps to ask for his approval for what I've done with his potential? Perhaps to seek his forgiveness for all I have not done? Would he like the middle-aged Tim, I wonder? Would he be pleased or disappointed to meet me here in the timeless moment?

In many ways, I still feel like an outsider from the world I see below me glowing in the darkness, full of other people who share this strange journey with me. I'm older, and my face shows the lines of my smiles and frowns. My life has been good and bad, exhilarating and terrifying, easy and hard. I have learned so much . . . and yet I know nothing.

As I sit here bathing in the warm night air, I feel washed by the ebb and flow of the polarities of existence. I'm immersed in the mystery and I'm contemplating my story. I have a timeless perspective on a temporary world. I'm the presence of awareness appreciating the show. I'm insignificant and vulnerable, yet magnificent and secure. I'm a transitory speck of cosmic dust, but I'm the star of the story of Tim.

Looking back, I see that I'm in love with my life. It has been a wonderful adventure, despite the heartaches and broken dreams. I'm now in my late 40s, becoming disillusioned and tired. Yet the child I once was is still here with me, full of innocent optimism, delighting in the play of forms. And all of the other Tims are here with me, too. I'm still traveling and arriving, as I was as a teenager. I'm still peering into the darkness in search of meaning, as I was in my 20s. I'm still on a mission to fulfill some half-guessed destiny, as I was in my 30s.

Will I ever understand this strange business called life? How can I when there's always more to see? If I live long enough, I expect that there will be plenty of unexpected twists in the story yet to come. I hope that I find I've been wrong many more times before the story of Tim reaches its last chapter.

What is life? I don't know. Yet the more enlivened I feel, the less I need to know and the more I want to rejoice and praise. All of my philosophical ideas, as the Zen masters say, are just fingers pointing at the moon. What is the moon? It's beyond words to express. But just look: How beautiful and mysterious it is. How bright and clear and glorious.

The finger become uninteresting when I see the moon. Words are superfluous when I get the meaning. When I feel this big love, I no longer need to analyze everything. I just want to hold the whole world in my careful hands like a newborn baby. When I taste how sweet it is to simply be, I just want to appreciate the miracle of the moment and dissolve into the mystery. I don't know what's going on. All I know is that I love it.

○ ○ ○

FURTHER RESOURCES

EXPERIENCE LUCID LIVING

To keep updated about Tim Freke's new books, stand-up philosophy shows, experiential seminars, and online events, join his e-mail list at: **www.timfreke.com**.

THE ALLIANCE FOR LUCID LIVING

The ALL is a deep awake community of individuals who share a passion for living lucidly. It exists to nurture the development of the new tribe arising at the cutting edge of evolution. To become a part of the ALL, contact: **theall@timothyfreke.com** or visit: **www.theall.org**.

ACKNOWLEDGMENTS

THANK YOU . . .

Anthony Taylor, for being the Director of the Alliance for Lucid Living, and for your immense clarity and creative insight in helping me write this book.

Debbie O'Shea-Freke, for your unconditional love, practical support, and gorgeous legs.

Peter Gandy, for your penetrating humor and grouchy wisdom.

Michelle Pilley, for coaxing this book out of me and being such a supportive commissioning editor.

Susan Mears, for being my literary agent, believing in me as a writer, and keeping me solvent.

All at Hay House, for being part of a very special publishing company.

Ellen Freke, for being my mum and a constant inspiration in the simplest of ways.

John Freke, for being my dad and encouraging my creativity.

Beau and Aya, for just being you.

And all of the beautiful human beings I have met during my adventures, with whom I have shared so much.

o   o   o

ABOUT THE AUTHOR

Tim Freke has an honors degree in philosophy and is an internationally respected authority on world spirituality, best known for his groundbreaking work on Christian Gnosticism. He is the author of many books, including *The Jesus Mysteries* (co-authored with Peter Gandy), which was a top-10 bestseller in the U.K. and the U.S., as well as a "Book of the Year" in the U.K.'s prestigious newspaper *The Daily Telegraph.*

Tim is also an innovative "stand-up philosopher"—a concept he developed from the ancient idea of a philosopher as a traveling "spiritual entertainer" who transformed people's consciousness. In his life-changing seminars, he shares profound ideas and practical techniques to help participants dive deeply into the ecstasy of being deep awake and living lucidly.

Tim is the founder of the Alliance for Lucid Living and on the board of advisors for Humanity's Team, organizations that are dedicated to our collective awakening. He is a clear and passionate communicator who is often featured in documentary films and talk shows broadcast by the global media such as the BBC and the History Channel.

Tim lives with his wife, Debbie, and their two children in Glastonbury, England.

www.timfreke.com

○ ○ ○

Hay House Titles of Related Interest

YOU CAN HEAL YOUR LIFE, the movie,
starring Louise L. Hay & Friends
(available as a 1-DVD program and an expanded 2-DVD set)
Watch the trailer at: **www.LouiseHayMovie.com**

THE SHIFT, the movie,
starring Dr. Wayne W. Dyer
(available as a 1-DVD program and an expanded 2-DVD set)
Watch the trailer at: **www.DyerMovie.com**

○ ○ ○

THE DIVINE MATRIX: Bridging Time, Space, Miracles, and Belief,
by Gregg Braden

THE FUTURE IS NOW: Timely Advice for Creating a Better World,
by His Holiness the 17th Gyalwang Karmapa Ogyen Trinley Dorje

INFINITE SELF: 33 Steps to Reclaiming Your Inner Power, by Stuart Wilde

*THE KEYS: Open the Door to True Empowerment and
Infinite Possibilities*, by Denise Marek and Sharon Quirt

*THE POWER OF INTENTION: Learning to Co-create
Your World Your Way*, by Dr. Wayne W. Dyer

RETURN TO THE SACRED: Ancient Pathways to Spiritual Awakening,
by Jonathan H. Ellerby, Ph.D.

*SUPERCHARGED TAOIST: An Amazing True Story to Inspire
You on Your Own Adventure*, by The Barefoot Doctor

UNDERSTANDING THE DALAI LAMA, edited by Rajiv Mehrotra

VISIONSEEKER: Shared Wisdom from the Place of Refuge,
by Hank Wesselman, Ph.D.

*WHO WOULD YOU BE WITHOUT YOUR STORY?
Dialogues with Byron Katie*, edited by Carol Williams

All of the above are available at your local bookstore,
or may be ordered by contacting Hay House (see next page).

○ ○ ○

○ ○ ○

We hope you enjoyed this Hay House book.
If you'd like to receive our online catalog featuring
additional information on Hay House books and products,
or if you'd like to find out more about the
Hay Foundation, please contact:

Hay House, Inc.
P.O. Box 5100
Carlsbad, CA 92018-5100

(760) 431-7695 or **(800) 654-5126**
(760) 431-6948 (fax) or **(800) 650-5115 (fax)**
www.hayhouse.com® • **www.hayfoundation.org**

○ ○ ○

Published and distributed in Australia by: Hay House Australia Pty. Ltd.,
18/36 Ralph St., Alexandria NSW 2015 • *Phone:* 612-9669-4299
Fax: 612-9669-4144 • www.hayhouse.com.au

Published and distributed in the United Kingdom by: Hay House UK, Ltd.,
292B Kensal Rd., London W10 5BE • *Phone:* 44-20-8962-1230
Fax: 44-20-8962-1239 • www.hayhouse.co.uk

Published and distributed in the Republic of South Africa by:
Hay House SA (Pty), Ltd., P.O. Box 990, Witkoppen 2068 • *Phone/Fax:*
27-11-467-8904 • info@hayhouse.co.za • www.hayhouse.co.za

Published in India by: Hay House Publishers India, Muskaan Complex,
Plot No. 3, B-2, Vasant Kunj, New Delhi 110 070 • *Phone:* 91-11-4176-1620
Fax: 91-11-4176-1630 • www.hayhouse.co.in

Distributed in Canada by: Raincoast, 9050 Shaughnessy St., Vancouver, B.C.
V6P 6E5 • *Phone:* (604) 323-7100 • *Fax:* (604) 323-2600 • www.raincoast.com

○ ○ ○

Take Your Soul on a Vacation

Visit **www.HealYourLife.com®** to regroup, recharge,
and reconnect with your own magnificence.
Featuring blogs, mind-body-spirit news, and
life-changing wisdom from Louise Hay and friends.

Visit **www.HealYourLife.com** today!